CW00672830

"In this vitally important book
unconscious shackles to the
made our culture so supreme
skill and poise he redirects us
divinity of nature which we sc
current global crisis. This won
for the mind and soul."

Dr Stephan Harding, Deep Ecology Research Fellow and
Senior Lecturer in Holistic Science, Schumacher College,
Dartington, UK

"Without attempting to psychologize religion, Julian David
in this fascinating, brief, yet scholarly enquiry into the history
of God, shares with the reader his deep understanding of the
psychology of the phenomenon, its underlying cultural,
mythopoetic origins and not least, the dark side of the
patriarchal politicization of religion and concept of God. To
me, it is a masterly 'once upon a time' story… an enquiry that
has something to do with you and me."

Ian McCallum, psychiatrist, analyst and author of *Ecological
Intelligence – Rediscovering Ourselves in Nature.*

This is a book which speaks up passionately for Nature
against the Law of Yahweh, beginning in *Genesis*, and the
consequent 'tragedy of patriarchy,' exploring how 'the
capacity to feel in an adult way has been stifled by thousands
of years of infantilisation by the One God.' Drawing on the
Sumerian myths of the Goddess, the story of Gilgamesh,
through Heracleitus and Nietzsche, and culminating in the
Greeks – Euripides' *Bacchae* and Sophocles' *Oedipus Rex* and
Oedipus at Colonus – Julian David reveals a hidden tradition
of reflection on how much we have lost, forever searching for
what is truly of value. His wise and gentle voice invites us to
consider the same question the Sphinx asked Oedipus: 'What
is a Man? What makes a human?' In the Nietzschean tradition
of the 'death of God,' it is tempting to wonder if this book
might become the 'death of Yahweh'?

Jules Cashford, Jungian analyst and author of
The Myth of the Goddess

"*A Brief History of God* is an absolute gem! Erudite, entertaining, and permeated throughout with that same profound blend of magic, mystery, razor-sharp intellect, and a feeling of aeons of impeccably archived wisdom that struck me on first meeting Julian in person.

"Julian David is a true elder, a wisdom-keeper, healer and storyteller of the kind I was privileged to have been mentored by during my growing up years in the wilderness of Southern Africa. Such elders are rare global treasures, and I am deeply grateful that the advent of mass-printed books will allow for his words to spread far and wide amid this time of confusion and destruction.

"The book deftly and fluently answers questions that are both pertinently historic and profoundly existential. Questions that I believe reach into the very heart of potentially understanding how we have come to the current critical state of social and environmental crisis. Questions, that in an ancestral culture such as those my mentors belonged to, are asked of us by they who went before, by the dead. Their unanswered questions are encoded in the old myths dating back to the very earliest dawning of our human history. No less today, at deeper, often unconscious levels, they confront every one of us in our dreams, as well as amid the archetypal realities that underlie and inform our daily living.

"In *Lament of the Dead: Psychology after Jung's Red Book*, co-author and Jung historian Sonu Shamdasani suggests that Jung came to the realisation that unless we come to terms with the dead we simply cannot live, and our life is dependent on finding answers to their unanswered questions. In *A Brief History of God*, Julian David articulates a narrative that in my view addresses just such vital ancestral questions."

Colin Campbell, African Medicine Doctor, Botswana and Cape Town

For Yasmin – my wife of 46 years and in the timeless

Julian David

A BRIEF HISTORY OF GOD

AUSTIN MACAULEY PUBLISHERS™

LONDON • CAMBRIDGE • NEW YORK • SHARJAH

A CIP catalogue record for this title is available from the British Library.

ISBN 9781528999717 (Paperback)
ISBN 9781528999724 (Hardback)
ISBN 9781528999731 (ePub e-book)

www.austinmacauley.com

First Published (2021)
Austin Macauley Publishers Ltd
25 Canada Square
Canary Wharf
London
E14 5LQ

Acknowledgements

Oliver Tringham, without whose support
I could not have written this book.

Table of Contents

I cannot define for human beings what God is. But what I can say is that my scientific work has proved that the pattern of god is present in every human being, and that this pattern has at its disposal the greatest transformative energy of which life is capable.

Carl Jung, in a letter to Laurens van der Post

When Albert Einstein announced that the electromagnetic field does not occur within space, but is the same thing as space, it started a long term change in our understanding, which is still seeping through the culture. No longer can space be thought of as passive. Rather, it hums perpetually, with energy, and everything that takes form in matter is composed of it…

But nothing comparable has happened in the vexed field of God. There was always a tradition within the formal religions, which felt Nature to be the manifestation of God, but it was muffled by the patriarchal nature of its theology. For whereas the male and female together are fundamental throughout Nature, no hint could be found of it in human politics. We have to accept that as late as the twentieth century here in England, the men who voted in our vaunted Democracy were psychologically only half-people, easily convinced that they needed their kings, and lords to look after them. And through all this the masculinity of God was beyond question.

But if we said now that 'God' did not make the world, for God, male and female, is the world, that God is the totality, the fact that anything is – let alone this world in its infinite wonders – and if even a part of the passion that has been poured out over the centuries by monks and anchorites and popes into a God who is a male creator, far above and beyond what He creates, could be poured instead into what exists, all would be saved, though not otherwise. For we have too long starved the world of what we alone can give it

The question is posed in the first two chapters of the Book of Genesis.

1 The Book of Genesis

In the beginning, God created the heaven and the earth.
And the earth was without form, and void; and dark-
ness was upon the face of the deep. And the Spirit of God
moved over the waters.
And God said, Let there be light: and there was light.
And God saw the light, that it was good: and God
divided the light from the darkness… and God saw that
it was good, very good.

These words are deep in the roots of our culture, including what is meant when God looks at the world and finds it 'good, very good.' A seed of optimism has been sown which will serve the culture well; and in the account of the creation which follows, no animal is created alone, ever, but always two by two; so that they feel in themselves the awesome power of creation — though only with another.

The name of God is not Lord Yahweh at this point, but Elohim, which is a dual name, neither male nor female but the energy that flows between them, so that it may be interpreted by ourselves now, as Mystery: in the sense that Einstein felt it in our own time as 'the most beautiful experience it is possible for us to know: the source of all true art and all science.'

The dual god in early Genesis probably dates from the time when the Hebrews had not fully separated off from the goddess religion of the peoples around them, with whom the goddess was never pure feminine but always the Two. And indeed, far, far ahead there would be the Dutch-Jewish philosopher called Baruch Spinoza (1640–77), for whom God and Nature were different words for the same thing, echoing much mystical writing, including that of the great Ibn al-A'rabi, at the peak of Muslim civilisation in the thirteenth century, when Europe was still in the grip of the idea of the One Father—though about to explode into the century of the great cathedrals, all built for the goddess and infant—as in the *hadith* chanted by his pupils:

> *I was a hidden treasure, and I created creatures that I could be known by them.*

The suggestions of a mutuality between God and Man were not pleasing to the Amsterdam Synagogue, which was firmly in the grip of the One God; but much worse would have happened to Spinoza anywhere in Catholic Europe, which was far more firmly in that grip. And today this is the only sort of thinking that nourishes the *feeling* that is crucial today for survival, both of humans and the earth itself. If the passionate energy that has been drawn away throughout the Christian era far, far beyond the skies, putting the Earth in grave peril, could be brought down and poured into the earth, both Earth and Man would come into a quite different relationship. It would be Love.

It would require an enormous development of the psychic function of Feeling, which Jung defined as the discernment of value. It is impossible to explain this in scientific language, but not more so than Einstein's feeling for the Mystery. It requires not Thinking but Feeling.

In our present world, Feeling is the last function to develop in the individual and almost impossible to explain in the language: particularly difficult to explain is Jung's insistence that Feeling is a *rational* function and part of the accurate perception of anything at all.

If we go back, however, to the time when Genesis was written, some time in the third millennium *BCE*, the Jews had

14

not fully separated from the goddess religion of the surrounding peoples, but soon would. For the long peace of the Neolithic was falling. Blond barbarians, hardened by the extreme conditions of the Russian Steppe, were pouring over the borders, killing the Neolithic men as they passed, and most of Old Europe went under. The Jews had no intention of going under; but they needed a different sort of God to survive. At verse 31 of Genesis, a voice rings out which is utterly different to Elohim. Feeling is not needed now, nor any experience of Mystery. The name of God is Yahweh, the Lord who makes Adam directly and has no feminine in him; and Adam is all male too. God plants up the Garden for Adam, and brings the animals to him to receive his lordship. Eve comes last of all, taken from Adam's own body in a reversal of how it is done in Nature. And if we ask ourselves how anyone could believe this *stuff*, the answer is that this is the coming of the world of power, when people will believe what their masters tell them. And that for the next three thousand years Elohim, who utters no commandments, forbids nothing and is concerned only with the Mystery that the world exists in its beauty — Elohim will drop away into the unconscious, though briefly born again with each new child that comes into the world.

And without Elohim, what is there left in religion? It is essentially a social obedience, backed up by images of punishment, which peaked in the most cruel and stupid religious concept ever conceived in the mind of man, which was Hellfire. We see that Genesis One is a natural document, since throughout Nature the sign of creation is always the two, never the One. And we see also that the male God has no interest in Nature and despises it, so that Eve is said to be taken out of Adam's body in defiance of how it is done in Nature, and the cry of the early Church Father Tertullian, 'credo quia impossibilis' (I believe *because* it is impossible), is the act of homage that the One God demands.

As the posturing of a tribal god, Yahweh would not matter to us now, except that he was spotted by an expanding empire in the first centuries of our era and adopted as the ideal God for Empire. And Constantine gave shape to this alliance in a series of Councils, presided over by himself and later his successors, charged with the task of deciding what everyone in the Empire must believe—on pain of *heresy*, which means 'choice,' from *haeresis*, the Greek word for that quintessentially human power, to choose. It was an admirably circular arrangement: the Church would support the Empire and the Empire support the Church; and no choice would be permitted in either. The vigorous sprouting of consciousness, so evident in Genesis One, would have no place here; and there would be no psychological development either, for obedience to Church, Empire and the One God was all that would be required from anyone.

When the Empire itself collapsed, as it had to, built on such a premise, the nation-states that grew slowly from the rubble would adopt the same symbols for themselves. In the reborn Europe, Czar would mean Caesar and so would Kaiser; there would be a Holy Roman Emperor at Vienna, and a representative of Yahweh himself in Rome. And over the Channel, the British would conclude, when their industry and commerce reached to the end of the world, that they were the true heirs of Rome, with the duty of teaching everyone how to live. And they would hold Anglican parades wherever they ruled in honour of the One God. And when, in 1914, with nowhere left to conquer, the Western empires fell on each other like dogs, in a very few years all were gone.

And the world was empty: no Czar, no Emperor, no *Duce* nor *Führer,* all of which had been surrogates for the same One God, whose role it was to lift from human shoulders the natural burden of being human and place it on a ruler in return for obedience. The sacrifice was in the realm of Feeling, which can only develop if that disburdening does *not* happen.

16

Thus the major at Auschwitz, when asked at Nuremberg what he *felt* when he gassed a group of 62 men, women and children, could reply that he felt nothing, at all: for he was ordered to kill these people in this way. And that, 'by the way,' he added, 'was how I was trained.'

The major is an eternal memorial to a humanity sacrificed on the altar of the One. And there were many on all sides of the endless conflict that it caused, who made the same sacrifice. But also some who didn't. In Bruges, there is a statue to another German officer who was ordered, during the invasion of Belgium, to destroy the city from the air. He disobeyed and was shot, but the city survived; and after the war, they erected this statue to him. During the re-conquest of Normandy, an English officer was ordered to bombard a French village prior to an attack by infantry. He knew that the enemy were already evacuating, and disobeyed. He was court-martialled and degraded, but the village survived, and after the war they asked him every summer, to visit.

Something has changed, something has ended: an era in human history perpetually torn apart by war, on which the future may look back and call the Era of the One.

2 Sumer

In the 1840s, an English traveller overland to India stopped at
Mosul, and hearing of mounds out in the desert collected
some men with picks and shovels and went out to investigate.
Hardly had they started, it seems, than they broke into a
series of caverns filled with baked clay tablets, many of them
broken and all of them covered with signs which suggested a
code. It was later identified as the library of an early king,
probably Sennacherib of Assyria, whose vast palace with its
hanging gardens had been close by. Sennacherib had ruled in
the first millennium *BCE*, whereas the tablets were inscribed
at least a thousand years earlier. The script was made up of
wedge-shaped marks made in tablets of damp clay with a
reed stylus and dried in the sun. It was effectively immortal
as the parchment and paper of later times could never be, and
the Sumerian culture that they described and brought up into
the light was at its peak in the early years of the third millennium, and suffered the general fate of Neolithic Europe.

Vast quantities of the tablets were shipped back to the
British Museum and soon all the major museums of the
Western world had some of their own. With this discovery
and the brilliant work of cryptology which followed, a completely unknown civilisation edged upwards out of the
shadows. It was the world as it might have been of Elohim,
before the invasions from the great Steppes of Asia destroyed
the civilisation which we now call Old Europe, and believe to

have been a peaceful goddess civilisation, tragically destroyed.

The great majority of the tablets were concerned with the normal business of any city; but there were also the rituals of the Temple, and the main festival there was the re-enactment of a marriage between themselves, the people, and their goddess Inanna, who was no individual person but Nature herself. The marriage established that relationship between man and nature in which each is in need of the other because they are opposites, and both are equal. It was the paradox on which any successful culture is based. The ritual began with a cry, ringing through an expectant silence. It is the goddess calling and this happens but once a year:

> *My womb, the horn, she cries,*
> *The boat of heaven*
> *Is eager like the young moon,*
> *My untilled land lies fallow…*
> *Who will plough my vulva, who will plough my high*
>   *field?*
> *and my wet ground?*

And the man who replies is called Dumuzi. Later, he will be Tammuz, later still Adonis, but always he is the son-lover and represents the people. He calls back:

> *Great Lady, I will plough your womb. I, Dumuzi the*
> *king, will plough your high field and your wet ground.*

And as the ritual proceeds, she is called down from her place in the eternal.

> *Come, they call to her,*
> *We have cleansed the rushes with cedar oil and made*
>   *them up into the great bed*

19

Inanna's reply is to come down and join in the preparation. She wants this marriage, and we see that there could be no creative end to it without this equality of her desire.

Soon she is bathing for the holy loins of Dumuzi, washing herself with soap, sprinkling sweet-smelling cedar oil on the ground, and at last...

> *The king goes with lifted head to the holy loins;*
> *Dumuzi goes with lifted head;*
> *Tenderly he caresses her, uttering words of love...*

I puzzled long on 'the lifted head,' but I think it is in this ritual because the bull and the he-goat both do it just like that when they approach the female at this time. Any farm-boy or -girl would know it well, and the Sumerians were all farm-boys or -girls. Soon, they would be working in the fields, which is really what this is all about, for the date for the enactment has been carefully chosen as the seventh day of the first moon after the winter solstice, when the soil is moist and ready for the seed, and the moon is in her boat-shape, which is also like an empty womb. And is she a young woman eager for love, or the young moon itself, or a goddess or all of them at once? There is no distinguishing Nature from Culture in this ritual. Both are parts of one felt reality. In our own culture, it would be labelled 'porn,' and it may have been performed literally in the Temple and qualify for that description, and maybe not. All we know is that there was then no war with Nature; and that the creator had not yet been masculinised, after which it would be merely absurd to plough him and seed him and make him fruitful. And we know too that in Sumer, the whole human, male and female, was still male in relation to Nature — and Nature was the timeless element in the relationship, the eternal.

This intimacy with Nature may be how they seem to us to have guessed things that modern science has only just arrived at, especially in the realm of dualities. At their processions in honour of the goddess, the men wore male clothing on their right side and female on the left and the women the other way round. They were honouring the bisexuality of the goddess but it was also their own experience of themselves.

Among the most entertaining and also profound of their myths recounts the visit of Inanna, the queen of the daytime, the sunshine, of love and joy, to her dark sister Ereshkigal in the Underworld. It begins…

> *From the Great Above, she opened her ear to the Great Below.*

It was as if she heard her sister calling inside her, and that both were ruling aspects of the same reality and needed each other. She must go, but she was also afraid that she might never come back, so first she gathered together all the things which shored up her upper-world identity. First, she placed the *shugurra,* the Crown of the Steppe, on her head. Then she arranged the dark locks of hair across her forehead, tied the small lapis beads around her neck, let the double strand of beads fall to her breast, wrapped the royal robe around her body, daubed her eyes with ointment called 'Let him come, let him come,' and bound the breastplate called 'Come man, come' around her chest. Lastly, she slipped the gold bracelet over her wrist and took the lapis measuring rod and line in her hand. With all this, she is as ready as she ever can be to make this visit to the opposite of all of it. But when she comes to the first of the seven gates of the *Kur,* the Underworld, the Chief Gatekeeper asks for her name and her business, and she replies that she is Inanna, Queen of Heaven, on her way to the East, the place of the sunrise and something she does every night.

The Gatekeeper is not impressed and replies:

21

*If you are truly Inanna on your way to the East, you
must wait here, for I must consult with my own queen.*

And when Ereshkigal hears about her sister, so apparelled,
she is annoyed, bites her lip, slaps her thigh, takes the matter
into her heart and dwells on it. Eventually, she says:

*Close all the gates, then open each one just a crack and
as Inanna passes through it, remove one by one her royal
apparel.*

And so it is done. And at each loss, Inanna protests in bewil-
derment:

What's this?

And the Gatekeeper admonishes her:

*Quiet, Inanna! The ways of the Kur are perfect. They
may not be questioned.*

Finally, at the seventh gate, her royal robe itself is taken off
and she arrives in her sister's throne-room completely naked;
and the judges of the underworld, the *annunka,* who are all
gathered there pronounce against her. Ereshkigal utters over
her the word of death, and Inanna dies and becomes a corpse,
a piece of rotting meat hanging on a hook.

The second half of the myth is about her return, but the
reader will have noticed that this is no primitive myth. To find
it in the most ancient script in the world turns all our ideas
about early societies upside down. Maybe the reader will
have noticed, too, the deep consciousness of how opposites
are twinned together, particularly life and the darkness from
which it comes, which is disliked by the male gods. For
Inanna has instructed her handmaid that if she doesn't return

soon, she should appeal to the male gods to help to bring her back. This shows a touching faith in the masculine that is greatly misplaced, for none of the male gods shows the slightest interest in getting Inanna back, except for one. The view of the others is that if she has chosen to cross the boundary into the other side, she should just stay there. They don't want to know about it—except Enki, the god of wisdom, who sees at once that a world without Inanna would be impossible. And his solution is of great interest, and not at all primitive.

He takes dirt from beneath his fingernail and fashions it into a small creature called a *kurgarra*, which is neither male nor female. Then he takes more dirt from under another fingernail, and fashions it into another little creature called a *gelatur* which is likewise neither male nor female; and he says to them both:

> *Go to the Kur, and creep through the door like flies. You will find Ereshkigal the Queen in the pains of childbirth, and when she cries out, 'ah, ah my side' do you cry out with her, 'aah, aah, my side, my side.' And when she cries 'aah! my heart, my heart,' you must cry with her, 'aah my heart;' and when she cries 'aah, aah my liver,' you will answer, 'aah! aah! my liver!'*

We can imagine the event in which this tale is told and that at this point, the whole audience would join in and cry, 'O my side,' and so on, and it would probably be the favourite bit of the story... until the queen stops. Someone has been sharing in her pain. The power of compassion, the suffering-with, has been activated. A new world is being born down there, some great renewal stirring in the depths, which could not have happened unless Inanna had made the first move and gone to find Ereshkigal. Now she wants to reward in some way, those who have come to share with her. She offers a conventional gift, the water-gift; and then another, the corn gift. But they have been told to accept nothing but the corpse that hangs on a hook in the *Kur;* which, as Ereshkigal finally admits, is her sister. So she gives it to them and Inanna rises up.

It is a story first told not later than the beginning of the third millennium *BCE*, and probably a great deal earlier. Yet it familiarises the whole culture with the single most intractable problem of modern psychology, which is the Shadow: that darkness and negativity, which is the companion of the world's great beauty, always has been and always will be.

Jung called it the Shadow. Nothing can truly exist without its Shadow. But he is not understood in our own culture. Whence comes this sheer wisdom, so far ahead of our own? It is an instinctual intimacy with Nature which they had never left.

We can only surmise the millions of years that humans no different from ourselves had lived with Nature, and *in* Nature, eating her nuts and her fruits, scratching the ground for her roots, occasionally killing one of her beasts and wondering at the strange intensity of its meat; and carrying all the while, the same crude, stone-age tools as their remote ancestors had carried millions of years back. For nothing changed. History had not begun. They knew that some great force had made the natural world with no help from anyone, and that it was infinitely above them and unchangeable.

This meant that both the people and this force were passive and had no thought of being other than they were. And this is still the quality of Nature. We do not know what happened inside the human for this to change, but in some way they came of age, and went where they had not dared to go: put their mattocks into her and quite soon their ploughs; and she was virgin no longer. And she responded, but not with outrage. It was as if she had waited for this through all the aeons of her development, that a creature born from herself had touched her with his *consciousness* and the doors of

24

her treasure house could be opened, bringing an undreamt-of increase in her fruitfulness. And history began. The human population increased exponentially: it was a new world and everything changed.

Where groups joined together, they found that the creative energy that flowed between them increased, too, exponentially, so that soon came the city, in which the ways that a man could develop, the skills he could invent, the people he could meet and work with multiplied enormously, until it became evident that the greatest gifts in the treasure house of Nature were within them, and the human imagination was harnessed to the creation of a new world. (Goethe was the first modern to understand this. 'A great building is a great work of Nature,' he wrote in *The Italian Journey*.) And this fundamental partnership with Nature was the key to every aspect of the wisdom of Sumer.

Tablets incised with the script have been found as far away as Cyprus and Greece, but it was here, in the lower basins of Tigris and Euphrates, that the foundations of our civilisation were laid down. We still have their 28-day moon, which are our months, and the seven-day quarter moon which are our weeks, and the sixty-minute hour and the sixty-second minute. And none of this was at all 'primitive,' though we can imagine that their measurements held them like a cat's cradle in the immensities of an unknown space-time; but soon came the first script.

It was trade that first made it necessary, the trade between the cities; and the decoding of even the small proportion of the tablets so far has revealed an extensive literature of poetry, temple rituals and myth, much of it concerned with Inanna and the depths of her love, as in the ritual of the Sacred Marriage between Nature and themselves.

But an inexorable fate awaited them. It was a civilisation grown entirely from the relation of humans to the Earth, stretching from the cities of southern Mesopotamia to the islands of Britain in the far North. But seen from the vast, cold landmass of Asia and its burgeoning population, it was no more than a warm, fertile peninsular, unprotected and ripe for the picking. The death of all that we have begun to know as Old Europe began in the third millennium *BCE*.

According to Thorkild Jakobsen, the great historian of Sumer, the fourth millennium and the ages before it had been moderately peaceful. Wars and raids were not unknown, but they were not constant and they did not dominate existence. In the third millennium, they appear to have become the order of the day. No one was safe. The quickness with which an enemy could strike — some warlord bound for loot to fill the long boats in which he moved along the network of canals criss-crossing Mesopotamia — made life, even for the wealthy and powerful, uncertain and insecure. Queens and great ladies, like their humble sisters, faced the constant possibility that the next day might find them widowed, torn from home and family and enslaved in some barbarous household.

This was not only a Mesopotamian disaster. The whole Neolithic world, which Marija Gimbutas was the first to interpret as a peaceful goddess culture tragically destroyed, suffered an overwhelming invasion by a completely different sort of human being. What is it that makes the human? It is perhaps the deepest question that confronts us.

I would say that it is the early experience of a kind earth. But on the great Steppe where the invaders had been bred, where ground temperatures might vary from fifty degrees in Summer to minus fifty in Winter, there would be no sense of that. A completely different sort of human being had broken into a civilisation that had flourished since its beginning, by means of a love between humans and the earth they came from; and these invaders understood nothing of it.

There are no written documents to help us with this vital period of history, but science has in part replaced them. First came radio-carbon dating, which told us the *when* of much that had before been lost in so-called 'pre-history.' More recently, came the tracing of DNA in burial places all over Europe, which have supplied a record of population changes in that tragic third millennium. Thus, it was around the mid millennium, 2,500 *BCE*, that Avebury, a thousand years in the construction, simply ceased to function. But we had to wait for the analysis of graves to know that there was an almost complete change in the population. Newgrange in Ireland went earlier, about 3000 *BCE* — probably because it was close to the shore and in the path of the longboats nosing around the tip of Scotland and falling upon the quiet undefended Irish coast.

At the same time, thousands of miles away in the lower basin of Tigris and Euphrates, the poetry of Sumer turned tragic.

> *Alas that day of mine, on which I was destroyed.*
> *For on that day he turned in the mountains*
> *into the road to me.*
> *For on it the boat came onto my river toward me*
> *For on it, heading toward me*
> *the boat moored at my quay*
> *For on it I the queen was taken on board in the stern,*
> *for on it I grew cold with most shivering fear*
> *for on it he yelled to me: Get up! Get on board.*
> *The foe trampled with his booted feet into my chamber*
> *the foe reached out his dirty hands towards me*
> *the foe stripped me of my robe, clothed his wife with it,*
> *cut my string of gems, hung it on his child,*
> *I myself was to tread the walks of his abode.*

While men like the master of this longboat harassed the waterways of Mesopotamia, other similar men poured over the boundaries into the unprotected garden that was Europe, and cut a swathe up to the northernmost point of Britain, killing the local men, as they went. That it was a real genocide, says Kristien Kristensen of Gottenberg University, is the only explanation of the fact that the men who built Stonehenge left no descendants.

The high civilisation which built Stonehenge and numberless smaller such monuments throughout Britain was destroyed specifically, it is thought, by a people called the Yamnaya, who came from the Eurasian Steppe, the area between the Crimea and the Carpathian Mountains, where the weather is particularly harsh. Later they morphed with the Beaker people, who were another branch of invaders from the East, and together they sank into the thousands of years of squalid hill-fort warfare that once we thought was our only inheritance. Stonehenge, however, is the central image in an unbearably tragic story. For of the civilisation that was destroyed, we know nothing. We can only ask questions. How did twenty-five-ton megaliths from a mountain in Western Wales come to Salisbury Plain? We can make guesses but there is no answer. Yet the unanswerable question how leads into another one which is actually more important. It is *Why*? Why did they do it? What was its 'purpose'? To which the answer must be: 'For its own sake and no other reason!'

And that signifies a completely different level of consciousness. Had they, perhaps, solved the economic problem, with a loved and fertile soil, treated as the partner in a marriage with plenty of surplus imagination and energy and no enemies? Could they then have turned themselves to the ultimate aims of civilisation, which is the freedom to do what are useless things for their own sake? They had no parchment or ink, and none of the sun-baked clay of the Sumerians; but they had granite in abundance. And five thousand years on, we are moved, as much as we would have been in the beginning, when we wander among the indestructible monuments that they left.

Meanwhile, the Yamnaya morphed with the Beaker people and the Corded Ware people. All originating in the great Asiatic steppes together, they descended into five thousand years of squalid hill-fort warfare, from which only the overwhelming fear of total destruction by nuclear weapons would at last deliver us. How can we use this quite unmerited gift?

Darwin was among the first signs of a culture about to break out from under the One God. His work on the Galapagos broke, in some way, a spell. The mutuality between the human intelligence and the world was quickly re-established, and within a century of Darwin's arrival on the islands, Einstein and the physicists were transforming our concepts of the Universe. What they found out there in the vast spaces they opened up was mystery upon mystery, both in the very small and in the very big, as if there would never be an end to it. And whereas all new thoughts and discoveries had previously been referred to Holy Scripture for judgement, with the real thing came images of unity between so many things that we had previously thought of as separate and discrete, that the ancient and intuitive striving for the unity of opposites seemed to be achieved at a stroke. Although all our worlds were turned upside down, we found that we could identify with the new one better than with the old, and feel that the fabric of the world was also the fabric of ourselves. It was the return of the imagination into Science, summoned there by Einstein for whom imagination was the first indicator of any intelligence; and a great healing of the wounds dealt by the patriarchal era seemed to be happening. And always in this new world we met the Two, nestling in the roots of existence.

This innate desire to cross over from the Nothing into Being is itself the Mystery. Where did it come from? What is this pressure out of the Beyond to come into Space, Time, Body? Why does the Electron *mind* if none other can be found to interact with it? Why does it care one way or the other? Why, when rejected, is it at once so ready to try again? And once that great crossing has been achieved, why does the same energy drive a lifetime on towards its own *end*, in Aristotle's sense of fulfilment? What is so special about *Being*, that men should cling to it?

Darwin had chosen the Galapagos Islands for many reasons, but principally because no one had been there. In that sense, it was still the world in which Genesis One was written, before the coming of Yahweh. Ultimately, he published the great *Origin of Species*, and no thunderbolt fell. Quite suddenly, the all-powerful, all-punishing God no longer existed, and the world lay open to speak simply of itself.

In 1913 Jung had a dream that he had to kill the hero:

> *I was with an unknown, dark-skinned man, a savage, in a lonely, rocky mountain landscape. It was before dawn. The Eastern sky was already light and the stars fading. Then I heard Siegfried's horn sounding over the mountains and I knew that we had to kill him. We were armed with rifles and lay in wait for him on a narrow path over the rocks.*
>
> *Then Siegfried appeared high on the crest in the first ray of the rising sun. On a chariot made of the bones of the dead he drove at furious speed down the precipitous slope. When he turned a corner we shot at him and he plunged down struck dead.*

Jung knew that he had to understand this dream. It was a matter of life and death, as much as that boyhood dream of Yahweh's turd falling on the cathedral in Basel, which he relates in *Memories, Dreams, Reflections*.

It was at the very end of 1913 and it was in the following year that he had the vision of a sea of blood covering the whole of Europe and wondered, was it a psychosis threatening himself, personally? Or what? In August, the war broke out and he knew. In five short years, Europe, as it then existed, destroyed itself and all its empires. It marked the end of a five-thousand-year era dominated by the ideal of emperor and hero. The recently discovered epic of Gilgamesh marked the beginning.

The historical Gilgamesh was king of Uruk in Sumer, the largest of that group of cities in the lower basin of the Tigris and Euphrates where our civilisation began. His story entered modern consciousness in the late nineteenth century, translated from the broken clay tablets found in great numbers beneath the sands of Iraq and inscribed in the earliest of any known human script. As it began to take shape, for there were many fragments and versions to piece together, the myth was greeted with increasing enthusiasm. Here was the authentic voice of Man as Hero, two thousand years before Homer. It began with a great hymn not to love, but to power:

> Surpassing all kings, powerful and tall
> Beyond all others, violent, splendid,
> A wild bull of a man, unvanquished leader,
> Hero in the front lines, beloved by his soldiers,
> Fortress, they call him, protector of the people,
> Raging flood that destroys all defences.

Strength is now far and away the dominant value, for the long peace of the Neolithic has been broken by the invasions from the East. From the opening of this poem, there are armies fighting, and the gods who preside over them are all male, or in the service of the male. So Arraru, the mother goddess of

31

creation, has put herself at the command of Anu the father God, and created a huge and perfect man...

> *The strongest of men — huge, handsome, radiant,*
>   *perfect.*

But the negative aspect of this beauty was there, too. Since he is the king, the female population belongs to him and the men who marry them are no more than temporary tenants, who stand aside at the weddings while he takes his due—for all maidenheads in Uruk are his. Since there is no power in the city to check him, he struts through it, trampling its citizens like a wild bull.

> *He takes the son from his father and crushes him,*
> *He takes the girl from her mother and uses her,*
> *The warrior's daughter, the young man's bride*
> *He uses her, no one dares to oppose him.*

So the people cry out and Anu commands Araru to make yet another man as strong as Gilgamesh, who will be his second self. Let them balance each other, he says, so Uruk has peace.

In Nature the male is balanced by the female, but something different is happening now, for a new reality is being constructed in which Nature will have no say whatsoever. So Araru makes another man of great size with muscles like iron, and puts him out in the desert to eat grass, run with the antelope, drink at the waterholes and have no knowledge of a human mother. And Gilgamesh will be told in a dream that this is his destined friend and helpmate, and set out to find him. Together they will form the first of those friendships between men which soon became the order of the day, for the first great test of male strength and virtue would be battle, and the second would be the games.

In the saga of Gilgamesh and Enkidu, once they had met there was no further mention of the love of women. Yet the historical Gilgamesh lived only a few centuries after the royal dynasties had begun in Uruk, which in itself marked the end of a much longer period in which the highest values had been feminine and also democratic, with the city governor no more than the first among equals. The point of change was around 3000 *BCE*, the same across the whole of the Mediterranean world, from Egypt and Mesopotamia to faraway Britain and Ireland, because it was in that century that the waves of giant, blond savages moved westwards and destroyed the long peace of that first civilisation. And by this time Uruk had become the most extensive city in the world.

The purpose of kingship was the protection of the people, but a heavy price was to be paid for it in the immense sense of value that was concentrated on the pharaoh or emperor, with a corresponding loss of value in the individual. In Uruk, as it had developed, the values were feminine and also democratic, which means personal. It was perhaps the most creative period in human history.

The Saga of Gilgamesh is like two streams meeting: the ancient goddess culture and the patriarchal revolution which overthrew it. We see this in the eventual meeting between the two outsize men in the incident of Shamhat, the Temple prostitute. For when Gilgamesh dreams of the giant man in the desert, who is his destined friend, he has a problem: how to get him out of the desert into the city, so that they can meet? It would be no good sending out troops to pull him in; he is far too big. So he sends a woman:

> *Go to the Temple*, he says, *and ask for a woman named Shamhat, one of the priestesses who give their bodies in honour of the Goddess. Take her out into the wilderness and when the animals come to the waterhole, and the wild man with them, let her take off her robe and lie*

there. Then he will approach her. Nature will take its
course and the wild animals will desert him.

And so it was done. She and the wild man made love for a
week and the wild man stayed erect throughout—at the end
of which he could no longer run with the antelope. But some-
how, his mind had expanded: he knew things that an animal
can't know. The key was the woman.

Now you know, she said, *what a woman is.*

In the culture of Sumer, the priestesses of the Temple were
the emissaries of the goddess, her stand-ins (which is actually
what 'prostitute' in our own language means, from the same
root as 'prosthesis'). In Shamhat's view, the *understanding* of
love is the point and meaning of the city. Enkidu's mind has
expanded; he knows things now that an animal cannot know,
and Shamhat considers that he is now ready for the city. And
she gives voice to a sort of hymn in praise of love.

> *Now that you know what a woman is*
> *Let me take you to the great city.*
> *I will lead you to Gilgamesh, the mighty king,*
> *You will see the great city with its mighty wall,*
> *You will see the young men dressed in their splendour,*
> *In the finest linen and embroidered wool,*
> *Brilliantly coloured with fringed shawls and wide belts.*
> *Every day is a festival in Uruk,*
> *With people singing and dancing in the streets,*
> *Musicians playing their lyres and drums, and*
> *The lovely priestesses standing before*
> *The temple of Ishtar, chatting and laughing,*
> *Flushed with sexual joy and ready*
> *To serve men's pleasure in honour of the goddess,*
> *So that even old men are aroused from their beds*

34

It is beautiful and also a little absurd, but Enkidu likes the sound of it, so they set off. But before they go, they meet a man who is on his way there to attend a wedding. He describes what will happen, how after the feasting and dancing, the bridegroom will step aside until the king has come to take his dues, and when he hears it, Enkidu begins to simmer and growl.

> *Who is this Gilgamesh, who does he think he is? I am the strongest.*

And when the great king arrives at the marriage house, Enkidu is standing across the door like a boulder and instantly they hurl themselves at each other, crack their great heads like bulls, fight up and down the streets, crashing into the walls of houses, until at last the king pins the wild man to the ground, and at once their rage disappears and they kiss and embrace and become real friends. And from that point on, we hear no more of maidenheads.

What is happening here, psychologically? It would seem to be a numinous experience so strong that it puts the love of woman into the shade. Woman-love has a different sort of numinosity: it is that of creation. This one is the power to destroy. How much cannot these two men destroy together? And as soon as their friendship is established, there is one enemy they must first conquer: it is Nature.

> *Now,* says the King, *we must go to the cedar forest, guarded by the great monster, Humbaba. We must kill him and drive evil from the world.*

Notice that Nature has taken up its accustomed place in a patriarchal culture: it is evil. Enkidu knows the sweet-smelling cedars that pierce the sky and stretch, he says, for a thousand miles. Humbaba's breath spews fire. He says:

His voice booms like thunder, his jaws are death.
He can hear all sounds in the forest, even
The faintest rustling among the leaves,
He will hear us a hundred miles away

It is a classic monster-myth at this point, where the monster is always Nature. Gilgamesh tells him not to be a coward, and when his own nerve fails, as it does along the way, Enkidu returns that support, so that they encourage each other. They go with the blessing of the entire city, which is avid for timber. It is a very different city from that described by Shamhat, but we don't expect consistency from this epic, since it is like two opposite streams meeting—and the strongest current is now for war. Gilgamesh's mother commends them, sends them out to win immortal 'glory.' Each carries outsize weapons and wears outsize armour, for they are outsize people, and it is only at a thousand miles that they pitch camp. Both have bad dreams on the journey, but both contrive to give positive interpretations to each other, so that they push on.

At last, they reach the great forest and at once meet the monster. After the initial boasts and gesturing, which were adequate to warn off ordinary humans, Humbaba realises that these men are his match and worthy of him. He offers to share the forest with them, which would be the solution of the old, feminine culture—man and Nature in a loving partnership. They can have all the wood they need, he says; but they must not kill him, for he is the appointed Guardian of the Forest.

Gilgamesh wants to accept this offer, but Enkidu, strangely, is dead against it.

Dear friend, quickly
Before another moment goes by,
Kill Humbaba, don't listen to his words

> *Don't hesitate, slit his throat,*
> *Before the great god Enlil can stop us.*

So they kill him and it is interesting that they are offending also the gods, and they know it…

> *At his death-roar the mountains of Lebanon split,*
> *The valleys ran with his blood for ten miles,*
> *The forest resounds. Then the two friends*
> *Slice him open, pulled out his intestines,*
> *Cut off his head with its knife-sharp teeth*
> *And horrible, bloodshot, staring eyes…*

The forest is now undefended. They take their axes and go further into it; and as they go, the wood chips fly:

> *Gilgamesh chopped down the mighty trees,*
> *Enkidu hewed the trunks into timbers.*
> *Enkidu said: By your great strength*
> *You have killed Humbaba, the forest's watchman.*
> *What could bring you dishonour now?*
> *We have chopped down the trees of the cedar forest.*
> *We have brought to earth the highest of the trees.*
> *The cedar whose top once pierced the skies.*

It is tragically from the cedar forests that the great rivers flow, which gave birth to the cities in the beginning, so the bell tolls for Sumer, too. In some few thousand years, the cities will sink into the sand and with them the vast clay-tablet libraries, to be found again only in our own time. In the same period, the verdant paradise of the Mediterranean, which was so many millions of years in the making, will be on its own way back towards the desert.

But now the friends are ready to go home. They build a raft and float it down the river to Uruk, Enkidu steering and

Gilgamesh holding the great head which they will lay up in some temple of the male gods; and when they arrive, Gilgamesh washes off the blood and filth of battle, puts on fine clothes and looks remarkably handsome, so that when the Goddess sees him, *her loins,* says the poem, *catch fire.* This, at last, is a man, she thinks, truly worthy of her.

When she courts Gilgamesh, she is doing no more than what Nature does to all of us, calls us to her, by her beauty, into a relationship with her. She wants what we have, which is consciousness, the outside point that only we can give her; and she wants to give us what she has, which is knowledge of the vast depth of matter; for she represents that which is opposite to the Spirit, yet mated with it. How much could we not do, she is saying, if only you would learn what a woman is. They could restore the destruction done in the forest, mend all the wounds inflicted upon her. But Gilgamesh spurns her utterly, and for two reasons. The first is, I believe, that she is useless in war. The culture she represents had lasted for thousands of years, but only because there were no enemies. Only Gilgamesh and others like him now can save the land. This is the reason for the string of vulgar insults that he hurls against the revered goddess:

> *Why should I wish to be the lover*
> *Of a broken oven that fails in the cold,*
> *A flimsy door that the wind blows through,*
> *A palace that falls on its staunchest defenders…*
> *A water-skin that is full of holes*
> *And leaks all over its bearer*
> *A piece of limestone that crumbles*
> *And undermines a solid stone wall…*

And so on, in the same vein.

The second reason for his scorn is deeper: it is a rejection of the great unifying myth of the Neolithic, that it is human to die. To know what a woman is, he must die.

> *Which of your husbands did you love forever?*
> *Remember what happened to that beautiful boy*
> *Tammuz: you loved him when you were both young,*
> *Then you changed, you sent him to the underworld*
> *And doomed him to be wailed forever.*
> *You loved the bright speckled roller bird and then you*
>   *changed…*
> *You loved the lion, matchless in strength, and then you*
>   *changed.*

And so on, through the catalogue in Sumerian myth of the Goddess-lovers. The whole natural world, human and animal, must die—which is exactly why she wants to join herself with it. She wants to know what it's like to *value* life, for which it is always necessary to have death waiting.

He says 'No,' but so rudely and contemptuously that she sends against him the Bull of Heaven. Down he comes tossing his horns; but the two men just pull him to pieces and throw back the bloody haunches in her face.

Or so the poem says. Actually, we can't kill the Bull of Heaven any more than we can kill Humbaba. We can only kill Humbaba within ourselves, and also the Bull of Heaven that will be sent to avenge him. Afterwards, they wash themselves in the river and go back to the palace hand in hand, calling out to the singing girls:

> *Tell me, who is the handsomest of men?*
> *Tell me, who is the bravest of heroes?*
> *Gilgamesh, he is the handsomest of men.*
> *Enkidu — he is the bravest of heroes.*

But in this conflict with Nature, the last card has still to be played. Enkidu dreams that because they have killed Humbaba, one of them must die—and knows it will be him; and that it will no longer be a kind return to the mother, but a thing of terror. It is the great turning-point in human history.

In Enkidu's dream, he is standing on a shadowy plain and...

> *A creature appeared with a lion's head*
> *His face was ghastly, he had a lion's*
> *Paws, an eagle's talons and wings.*
> *He flew at me, he seized me by the hair.*
> *I tried to struggle but with one blow,*
> *He capsized me like a raft, he leaped*
> *Upon me, like a bull he trampled my bones.*
> *'Gilgamesh, save me, save me,' I cried.*
> *But you didn't save me. You were afraid and you*
>   *didn't come.*

In the house of the Dead, where he is taken...

> *All who enter*
> *Never return to the sweet earth again.*
> *Those who dwell there squat in darkness*
> *Dirt is their food, their drink is clay,*
> *They are dressed in feathered garments like birds,*
> *They never see light and on door and bolt,*
> *The dust lies thick.*

The relationship of man to death has utterly changed, and with it his relation to Nature and his own unconscious nature. And as soon as Gilgamesh has buried Enkidu, he goes into the desert with matted hair and a lion-skin, to wander there, weeping; but it is his own mortality that he weeps for:

Must I die too? Must I be as lifeless
As Enkidu? How can I bear this sorrow
That gnaws at my belly, this fear of death
That restlessly drives me on? If only I
Could find the one man whom the gods made immortal
I would ask him how to overcome death.

The one he looks for is Utnapishtim, known to us as Noah, part of that bit in Hebrew mythology that had its origin in Sumer. It is Utnapishtim now who built the ark, came through the Flood and had been granted, in Sumerian myth, eternal life for doing so. The rest of the poem is devoted to Gilgamesh's search for that elusive thing.

There are many incidents as Gilgamesh wanders through the world, all of them recounted with the wit, humour and understanding of the early poet. One such is when he encounters a woman who brews beer and keeps a tavern; and she is deeply shocked by the state he is in. It is not normal for her visitors to be unwashed, unfed, burnt by the sun and blistered by the cold. How can this be, she asks?

How can it not be, he answers? How can it not be, since my friend is dead and I will have to die myself? And she says: what sort of madness is this? And she gives him the philosophy of the Goddess culture, much as Shamhat gave it to Enkidu. Eternal life is gained by the complete living of this one:

Humans are born, they live, then they die.
That is the order that the gods have decreed.
… Enjoy your life,
Spend it in happiness not despair.
Savour your food, make each of your days
A delight, bathe and anoint yourself,
Wear bright clothes that are sparkling clean,
Let music and dancing fill your house,

Love the child who holds you by the hand
And give your wife pleasure in your embrace.
That is the best way for a man to live.

But Gilgamesh is not comforted. Another significant incident follows hard upon it, for the tavern-keeper suggests that, if he is so determined to get across the great ocean of death, he try Utnapishtim's boatman, who is close by and he has his oarsmen with him. The oarsmen are made of stone, and so can pass through the fire that is in the middle of the ocean. Perhaps they can help him. Gilgamesh's reply is to grip his axe, draw his knife, creep up on them and when he is close, give a great battle-cry and fall upon them so furiously that the stone men are all broken and fall into the water. It is a curious way, the poet thinks, to approach people whom you hope will help you, but it is Gilgamesh's way. He has cut himself off completely from the opposite principle, which is represented by the Goddess. He just doesn't know what it is. After many vicissitudes, however, he does make it across the ocean, through sheer trying, and Utnapishtim tells him the story of the making of the Ark. Utnapishtim too is as shocked by his appearance and his attitudes as the tavern-keeper had been, and gives him the same advice. But Gilgamesh is, of course, unmoved. So Utnapishtim hits on a piece of theatre which he thinks might get through to him.

What have you done, he asks, that might incline the gods
to grant you eternal life?

Utnapishtim himself has done a lot, built a ship that can survive the waters, gathered together the whole instinctual world into his ark.

Build then the ship of death, says D. H. Lawrence.

This man has built his. What has Gilgamesh done? Nothing so far. It is a matter of consciousness so Utnapishtim sets a test for him. Stay awake, he says, for a whole week, and then maybe the gods will grant you eternal life.

Gilgamesh is quite sure he can do it, and he wants to start at once; but in reality, he can't do it for a single minute. He sits down against a wall to begin, and is at once asleep. Utnapishtim knows that he will not even know that he has been asleep and certainly won't admit it. So he asks his wife to bake a loaf for each day that their visitor stays asleep. On the last of the seven days, he touches him, and Gilgamesh wakes up with a start. 'I was nearly asleep when you touched me,' he says. And Utnapishtim leads him to see that the first loaves are already mildewed, while even the newest is past its best, for bread must be eaten fresh, in the moment, like life itself which is what this part of the myth is really meaning. And Gilgamesh, at last, accepts it. It is the first bit of self-knowledge that he has ever had; and he is able now to start the long journey back to where he started, which is Uruk.

The poem ends with a hymn in praise of the city and all that it means:

> *This is the city of Uruk,*
> *Which no city on earth can equal.*
> *See how its ramparts gleam like copper in the sun.*
> *Climb the stone staircase more ancient than the mind*
>   *can imagine.*
> *Approach the Eanna temple sacred to Ishtar*
> *A temple that no king has equalled in size or beauty*
> *Walk on the wall of Uruk, follow its course*
> *Around the city, inspect its mighty foundations*
> *Examine its brickwork, how masterfully it is built,*
> *Observe the land it encloses, the palm trees, the*
>   *gardens,*

> *The orchards, the glorious palaces and temples, the*
> *shops*
> *And market places, the houses, the public squares…*

But not even the writer could know that, though men like Gilgamesh had built the wall, they had not built the city that it protected. That had grown through two thousand years of trade, invention and the skilful tillage of the earth; out of a myth of which Gilgamesh knew nothing, that of the Neolithic Goddess who was the all-nourishing earth herself.

3 Heraclitus and the
Beginnings of Science

Some twenty-five centuries ago in Athens, the Western psyche had to absorb the impact of Logic, founded on a premise as much opposed to Nature as Yahweh had been for the Jews: it was that opposites exclude each other; and on this, the whole structure of formal logic was erected. In Nature, of course, opposites need each other, seek through the world to find each other, because they seek always for the Whole. Jung called 'wholeness' the god-image in the psyche. In logic, of course, there is no such thing as a Whole and there is no mention of it in any scientific lecture-room. But when, in the New Mexico desert, we split the atom to make a Bomb, we reversed the process by which Nature had built itself up over millions of years, which was always by accretion. In the great explosion which was the final achievement of our work, an unquantifiable energy was set free which we used for destruction. But at that moment, too, the world started to heal, for that is what a live organism does. In the desolation of the post-war world, the life sciences (psychology, ecology, ethology and the rest) burst into Being, bringing with them a totally different sort of thinking which Logic had driven from the field; and we realised the reason of why we knew nothing of Nature. It was because our contact with the language in which it speaks had been severed and we were out of touch. In synchronicity with this realisation, Science discovered the physical existence of two hemispheres in the brain, which

45

raised at once the question: what would a complete human language look like?

Heraclitus was contemporary with the beginning of science in the Athens Academy, and he watched it from across the Bosphorus at Ephesus with deep misgivings – because Science (which is the study of *how the world is*) was becoming identical with Logic, and the world isn't logical. It was curiously like what James Lovelock, in the twenty-first century, is telling Science, for Science has not changed its heart. It would much prefer a world that behaved like a machine, in which we could do the same experiment a hundred times and it would return the same answer.

> *But*, said Heraclitus, *we do not step twice in the same river.*

Neither do opposites exclude each other.

> *Without high and low notes there would be no music, and without male and female, no animals, both of which are opposites.*

Heraclitus, we can see now, was a right-brain thinker. The scientists called him 'obscure,' which is the common fate of right-brain thinkers; but they could never quite dismiss him, because they all had their own right hemispheres, however deeply they had been buried. But he spoke continuously of the things that Logic could not encompass.

> *All is Flux*, he said.

The source of systematised Logic was Aristotle, who became the revered father of modern science. But long before their 'discovery' in our own time, he knew the two hemispheres, because both were alive within him and he had needed to distinguish between them. The illusion that Logic can be applied to Nature was not possible for him, for as well as two sorts of thinking, there were two sorts of Being. The word for *Being* in Greek is *ontos,* as in *ontology* and many other of our words; and for Aristotle there were two sorts of Being in the world and two distinct causalities. There are things, which are produced by human planning and execution, such as tables or chariots, or houses. This he called the *tekne onta:* and there were the things of Nature, that which produce themselves by *rising out of themselves.* Logic belongs to the first, but not the second. The second is the mystical tradition of Nature as *epiphania,* the making of what is inside manifest. We might call it 'God'; Einstein called it the Mystery, and appealed to its beauty and its place as source and origin. Aristotle, too, had his own feet in that mystery, and felt about it in much the same way. He knew the two hemispheres in the best way they can be known: that both were active inside him. It was his greatness as a thinker, and his tragedy (and ours) that no one followed him, or even tried to follow, because the social pressure from left-brain thinking among students was so extreme, as it has been ever since. For Aristotle, the ceaseless advance of everything, plant or animal or insect, towards its full manifestation was the energy of creation itself. It *corresponded* to the cause-and-effect of human activity but it came from within.

The studies of Konrad Lorenz in the twentieth century were the main element in the explosion of the life-sciences after the war: because he watched that life-energy, observed it, took notes and wrote them up. They showed Nature as entirely capable of looking after itself, because following a mysterious guide which we called instinct, which we used to look down upon, because we thought that Logic must be superior. Yet this is creation and Logic never created anything; and after a war, in which the whole world had come close to utter destruction, we learnt how much better instinct would have handled it. For example, in a battle between wolves, the weaker need only bare his throat, for the stronger to be barred *by instinct* from harming him. Thus precedence is established, which is necessary for the pack and the pack doesn't lose a wolf. It was a rational solution to the problem of aggression, *and the voice that spoke through it was always the Whole, the wholeness of the pack, the wholeness of the individual, the wholeness of the world beyond.*

A change was required in the concept of instinct, so profound that it had to include an element similar to the *Anima Mundi* of the alchemists. It was felt necessary that it should come from Science itself, and it was not long delayed. It came in Lovelock's *Gaia Hypothesis,* which demanded that the world be considered not so much as a machine, but as a self-regulating organism. Most practising scientists rejected the hypothesis, and it would require a great re-adjustment to accept it. Instinct would have to be considered as a network of *higher consciousness* running through the world, taking the voice of the Wholeness of things into every corner, so that a herd of antelope might graze in sight of a feasting lioness, since they would 'know' that she has had one of them and they are safe for a while. If the instinct of the animals could become conscious in the human (which is more possible than we think, since we are animals too), the world might be saved — but not otherwise. And though the magnitude of the change demanded on every level is enormous, it is only Nature breaking in, at last, upon a culture long paralysed by pressure from Yahweh.

Heraclitus and the Logos

Heraclitus lived before Yahweh and Logic had settled together on the European mind like a curse; for both Yahweh and Logic were separate from Nature and opposed to it. With

Heraclitus, we are back on the ground level of human consciousness, the world eloquent simply of itself. That speaking world was what Heraclitus meant by the 'Logos.'

The word 'Logos' comes from the Greek *legein,* to speak, and this was the speaking of Nature, and it could equally be thought of as the speaking of God. For Heraclitus, it was holy because Nature itself was holy. And it is expressed in images, which is how it was expressed to us, when first as children, we opened our eyes upon it. Which is probably what Jesus meant when he said:

> *Unless you become as little children you cannot enter the kingdom of Heaven.*

And in the same discourse:

> *Consider the flowers of the field. They neither spin nor reap but Solomon in all his glory was not arrayed such as these.*

We can imagine him so clearly picking a flower and just making the apostles *look. To look* into the heart of a flower is extremely difficult. It is the Mystery itself; as Eliot learnt (probably in the writing of the *Four Quartets* which goes extremely deep) that 'Humankind cannot bear very much reality.'

Sensing the millennia of arid academia stretching ahead in the colleges and universities by which the world's own voice would be drowned out, Heraclitus stated the naked empirical principle:

> *Whatever comes from sight learning from experience, this I prefer.*

At the other end of the desert that separated him from our own time, Ludwig Wittgenstein in 1916, sitting in an Austrian trench writing in a small notebook what would become the *Tractatus Logico-Philosophicus*, picked up the same gauntlet and wrote:

> *A proposition in logic has no content. Any attempt to make it seem as if it had content is false.*

Later, back lecturing in Cambridge, he countered philosophy's search for the 'crystal purity of logic,' with an image:

> *We have got onto slippery ice where there is no friction and so in a certain sense the conditions are ideal, but also, just because of that, we are unable to walk. We want to walk so we need friction. Back to the rough ground!*

The frictionless movement of logic is a perpetual temptation to all of us. But its pleasure can exist only in abstraction. It cannot be found in the world. Wittgenstein's students were greatly attracted by his personality, and his lectures were crowded. But very few of them guessed what he was trying to do. The philosopher G. E. Moore had an inkling. In his notes on Wittgenstein's 1933 lectures, he wrote:

> *Wittgenstein believed his 'new method' to require a sort of thinking to which we are not accustomed, in which we have not been trained, a sort of thinking very different to what is required in the sciences.*

Where do you go if you let go of the lifebelt of Logic? There is nowhere to go except the world itself.

Heraclitus was an enigma to the mainstream of his own time, as Wittgenstein was to his. Both were felt as 'dark,' 'riddling,' something one would like to be able to dismiss, but

couldn't quite. The problem was that we need both hemispheres to read either of them. In effect, this meant both spoke
to the imagination as well as to the intellect. One has the
impression that Heraclitus is using language as much for its
shapes and textures as its meaning, or rather that its meaning
is in those shapes and textures: and chiming through the fragments which survive, always the harmonies of opposites, as
in any organism:

> *There would be no music without high and low notes
> and no animals without male and female, both of which
> are opposites.*

Wittgenstein was using imagery too, describing philosophy
in terms of the narrow, twisting streets of an ancient city-
centre, with the broad, straight boulevards out beyond. He is
coming very close to Heraclitus in such moments without
ever mentioning him or probably reading him, for neither
was a great student of other philosophies. With Wittgenstein,
it was more likely that he would turn to a fairy tale.

Heraclitus was the first to use the word 'psyche' in the
way we use it now:

> *You will not reach the limits of the soul (psyche) by
> going, even if you travel over every way, so deep is its
> logos.*

He was also, for two and a half millennia, the *last* to use the
word in that way. He was the first psychologist, and for thousands of years, also the last; for it was the wholeness of the
psyche itself which was lost in the long, desert years.

Even in the darkest times, however, his Logos was established at the heart of the Christian world, and here I would
ask the reader's somewhat solemn attention (and maybe their
patience too). It was placed here by an intricate chain of

synchronicity, which always announces the approach of the Mystery. It was the opening of the Gospel of St John, appointed to be read (by what inspiration we do not know) at the end of every Mass in the world. It was called the Last Gospel, as if it summed up everything else, and it starts like this.

> *In the Beginning was the Word. And the Word was with God and the Word was God. And through the Word was everything made and without it was nothing made that was made.*

'The Word' was Logos in the Greek, and it was the Heraclitean Logos, not the Platonic one, for it is not about the process of thinking, but about the world itself.

Translated into Latin, however, Logos becomes *verbum*; and taken further on into English it becomes *Word*; but neither has the organic, rooted quality of the Logos. And it was quite illogical, for how can anything be *with* something else *(apud Deum)* and also the same thing? We dismissed it as nonsense, though interesting nonsense; and one day someone would see that it was not about logic at all, but about Being. And then he would be in a different mental world, that of Heraclitus.

He might even think back to that so-distant moment when the long-established peace of a dead piece of rock circling the sun was shattered by a cell which split into two and remained one. This is not possible in Logic, but happens, of course, in the organism. It is the logos of life. Soon it would be many cells and still one. Ultimately, it would be a whole world, and Heraclitus would say:

> *Listening not to me but to the Logos, it is wise to agree that all is One.*

It is an unaccustomed grammar, so we may miss its point, which is that: the All is also One. It doesn't stop being the All. And now, the rest of the passage follows naturally, for we have the key:

> *Through the Logos everything was made, and without it was nothing made that was made.*

Had the two modes of thought, Logic and the Logos, been able to marry in the mind (and the two hemispheres were ready and waiting), a long destined intelligence might have been born. Maybe it is still there, in the future, for the two hemispheres are still waiting. But since the point of marriage is to make the Whole out of the Two, and be still Two, we may not expect that either Logic or Yahweh will have a part in it.

Both, however, are the mainstay of the life-studies (psychology, ethology and the rest) that have at last broken through. We have the beginnings of a rebuilt world, and Elohim is still there.

4 The Tragedy of the Patriarchy

In a very brilliant book (the author's *first* book) called *The Birth of Tragedy*, Friedrich Nietzsche describes the fertility cults of the Pelasgian peoples who surrounded the Greeks and survived among them as a peasant underclass, occasionally erupting into a great Festival which celebrated fertility itself, which was for the Greeks a matter of disgust and alarm.

> *Almost universally the centre of these festivals was an extravagant lack of sexual discipline, whose waves engulfed all the venerable rules of family life. The most savage beasts of nature were here unleashed, even that repellent mixture of lust and cruelty that I have held to be a witch's brew...*

The problem is, how did Nietzsche know about this — for he certainly wasn't there? Yet his tone is familiar to us from the Hebrew prophets, for whom the Fertility Festivals of the neighbours were the greatest abominations possible; and the prophets weren't there either. Their response has the marks of a projection, therefore, of great power and virulence, and that itself is the tragedy. It was the alienation of the human psyche from Nature. The Jews under Abraham had trekked out of the fertile culture of Sumer, the centre of the ancient Goddess civilisation, to find a Father God who apparently came to Abraham in his dreams and commanded it. They went to serve a God who was male alone (for the Goddess was always dual) and would be a leader in war. Again and again, they met the old religion, which was spread all over the Neolithic world, and he would order a war or even a genocide rather than risk an inter-marriage.

Historical evidence is sparse, but the movement of Aryan tribes from the North down into the Greek peninsular in the first millennium *BCE*, led by the horse-drawn chariots which were the Panzer tanks of the time and easily overcame the agrarian peoples they passed among, was like the exit of Abraham from Sumer, though technologically far in advance. What they had in common with the Jews was their worship. Their gods were warrior sky-gods, very like the Yahweh God of the Jews; and the ancient love-relationship between the Goddess, who was the Earth itself, and the humans who were born from her, was strange to them and rather repulsive. In the tale from Ovid, Apollo is boasting how much better an archer he is than little Eros, for he has just killed the great female serpent who protected the Mother sanctuary at Delphi. Eros was the child of the Goddess and his work was love. The invaders were better at killing. They had mastered the Bronze Age technologies in the North, had learnt to sink mines for minerals, and how to make slaves work in them and more slaves to hammer and smelt the alloy of tin and copper, which made their all-conquering weapons. They had learnt, too, to cut great blocks of stone for building walls and cities. They had needed slaves for that, and had known how to get them. Slavery was as necessary to them as petrol is for us; and when, in our own time, an Aryan warlord arose once more, speaking of conquered peoples as natural slaves, he spoke proudly from the Aryan tradition.

Yet the roots of the culture were always in tragedy for Apollo failed catastrophically in love, leaving Eros with the last word. According to Ovid, Eros had two arrows, one of which was golden and excited love, while the other was leaden, and caused revulsion. He took a golden tip and shot it into the thigh of Apollo, just as Daphne came in sight: and Apollo was possessed by a longing for a wholeness he had only just realised was possible, but seemed now all that mattered. Then Eros took a leaden tip and shot it into Daphne, who was filled with horror for this man who thought he could possess her by conquest. Apollo went after her, like the hound after the hare, but she merged back into the Nature from which all the nymphs had only half-emerged. And Apollo might analyse her, dissect her, shine his bright light upon her, but never know her. For the nymphs are in no part of Nature but only the whole.

The woods and streams around Delphi were full of nymphs who were escaping from Apollo. In future centuries, the old, agrarian Europe would be steadily remodelled in the image of Apollo. The tillers of the soil would be no longer partners of the eternal, but the serfs and peasants of Aryan masters. In time, they would be the titled and escutcheoned knights of Europe; but the woods would still be peopled by nymphs who had fled from them, back into trees or flowers or pools of water. They longed to woo them, but they were very stupid where nymphs were concerned. Their fate was to be isolated from their own depths, like plants pulled out of the earth, their roots waving in the air, fast drying out: seeking nourishment where there was none to be gained.

By Nietzsche's time, Apollo was an allegory for Science, the symbol of a Nature redeemed from itself by conquest. Apollo would shine his light, it was thought, into its darkest corners and its power would be destroyed.

> *To the febrile excitement of these festivals, knowledge of which came to the Greeks along every route of land and sea, the figure of Apollo rose up in all its pride and held up the Gorgon's head to the grotesque, barbarian Dionysian, the most dangerous force it had to contend with.*

The Gorgon's head was feminine, but serpents coiled about it instead of hair; and her face was supposedly so ugly that any man or woman who looked upon her would be turned to stone. Perseus, another solar hero, had gone down to find her. Assisted by Athena, who lent him her shield for a mirror, he had severed the head and brought it back to the upper world, where it ended up on Athena's shield. Athena was the virginal feminine, but powerfully so, both armed and armoured, born from Zeus' head, with no female womb intervening. This capture of the Underworld terror and turning it against itself was, for Nietzsche, the great achievement of Greek culture.

But there was another explanation for the Gorgon's ugliness, and psychologically it was the more pertinent. It came from the folk-tradition of the old mother-culture which had continued in counterpoint with the new myths of the conquerors, somewhat as the tales collected by the Grimm Brothers continued in Europe, providing a rich quarry for psychology. In this tradition, the Gorgon was indeed ugly, but had not been born so, quite the contrary. She and her sisters had been as lovely as the Three Graces themselves, unfortunate only in the attention of Poseidon, one of that triumvirate of Father-Gods who ruled the patriarchal world. Poseidon had raped her in the temple of Athene. But Athene had not punished him. They were fundamentally good friends, though he was probably annoyed by her stubborn virginity. But the real culprit was beauty itself, so Athena cursed that; and a visit to the red-light areas in any of the cities of the patriarchy will show what the curse has done to the lovely acts of generation.

When Euripides (the subject of the next chapter) came to write his first play, *Medea,* it was the start of a long life dedicated entirely to making Athenians conscious of their sisters. The Greek tragic theatre was the greatest consciousness-making institution invented by any human society; but his was a life-work that failed. The people loved the poetry, for they took great pride in their language, but their patriotism drowned out his meaning. Only four or five times in a long life did they vote him the first prize at the Festival. Towards the end, as the Peloponnesian War dragged on, he grew more and more unpopular in Athens, until his last and greatest plays were written in exile, in a remote valley in Macedonia.

Medea herself was a figure to match the Gorgon, having killed her children for motives, they said, of sexual jealousy—which women were not permitted to feel. She had brought the most beautiful symbol of the heart's desire to Greece. It was the Golden Fleece—and Jason, who had seized it, was guided each step of the way by her.

Medea had loved the young adventurer as soon as she saw him. She saw a world ahead of a courage that alone could be worthy of the Fleece, in which people would grow into themselves outside the cruel monarchy which held it as its prisoner. Her offer to help him was also a determination to go with him, to breed children with him, create a world with him. Jason, we can imagine, swore by every god it was possible to swear by, that he would do it with her. Instead, once they were back in Greece, he was at once a hero, and a fit son-in-law for a king of Corinth; while she was an embarrassment in polite society, a concubine brought from a far and savage place, their children illegitimate. The love that brought the Golden Fleece and made the children was already betrayed. The words that Euripides puts in Jason's mouth are reasonable, intelligent and utterly uncomprehending of her passion. Euripides, in his first play, goes straight for civilisation's greatest problem: that the power to create in the feminine is of just the same intensity as its power to destroy; and they had installed it in the heart of their homes. There was no comforting pretence, either, that it could be killed by some hero and put on the shield of Athene. It would remain where it was until men took notice, which, twenty-five centuries later, still hasn't happened. Shelley picked it up in early nineteenth-century England, and only his genius could make its horror suddenly true for us.

> *Can man be free if woman be a slave?…*
> *… In their home,*
> *Among their babes, thou know'st a curse would wear*
> *The shape of woman.*[1]

Like the story of Medea itself, it strikes to the heart, and we can scarcely look on it. Neither Euripides nor Shelley leaves it there. Both bring us back to the question: what do civilised men (and women) do to their own nature? And that itself is the tragedy of the patriarchy.

Theseus, the founding hero of the Greek world, had behaved in just the same way in Crete. Athens had been bound, it was said, to a certain tribute to King Minos of Crete. It was seven youths and seven maidens, to be sent at nine-year intervals as food for a certain monster, half-man half-bull, kept in a labyrinth beneath the King's palace at Knossos. The children were generally chosen by lot, but Theseus, the king's son, chose to be one of them; and when they arrived at Knossos, he chose also to be the first to be fed into the labyrinth—at which point Ariadne, Minos' daughter, fell in love with him, just as did Medea with Jason. For Love has its own energy, its own drive towards creation; and it was for love that she must smuggle his sword to him and also a ball of string, which he must unravel behind him as he penetrated into the labyrinth, while she held the other end, so that when he had found and killed the beast, he could find his way back to her. Her only condition was that he would take her with him back to Athens, where they would found this new world of love. Theseus finds and kills the monster and escapes with

---

[1] Percy Bysshe Shelley, *The Revolt of Islam, Canto Second, XLIII.*

all the youths and maidens, and also Ariadne. They reach the Isle of Naxos and put in for water, and to roast an animal or two upon the beach. Ariadne goes to sleep — it has been a long day — but wakes alone, with Theseus a distant sail on the horizon. He has tricked her.

She took no revenge, but all would not be well with Theseus, especially where women were concerned. He forgot the promise he made to his father — that if he came home with the Monster dead, he would change the black sails he set out with, for white ones. He forgot and his father, believing him dead, cast himself down from the Acropolis into the sea, which must have been closer then. Theseus takes over, but his reign is marked throughout by a rooted stupidity in regard to women. His only happy union is with Hypolita, the Queen of the Amazons — who fought with him in all his battles, and bore him Hippolytus — on whom Theseus, misled by a later wife into believing he had raped her, utters so terrible a curse that the youth crashes his chariot and is killed.

With Ariadne, we feel that he might have awoken a real connection with Nature, which instead he betrayed. And the very beautiful image of the labyrinth — with Ariadne holding the thread outside, and Theseus returning to her along it — is incongruent with that other image: Ariadne left asleep on the shore at Naxos, while Theseus sails home to Athens without her.

5 Euripides

The Women of Troy

The destruction that faces the whole world in our own time faced Greece in the time of Euripides, but on a smaller scale — the bowl of the Mediterranean. The bones of their marvellous cities still lie scattered around its shores, and behind them are the barren hills and valleys where rain once fell, trees grew and corn was harvested as splendid as the cities. But in a single sea-battle, a whole forest could sink to the bottom, and their battles were constant. The seventy-four years of Euripides' life spanned the period in Athens when the idea of empire hung over the city and tempted it towards its own destruction; and while the philosophers and playwrights were creating the first truly great literature in the world, the majority of the citizens were showing themselves capable of any crime in the interests of conquest.

In 430 *BCE*, there opened the long war with Sparta that would last for thirty years and end in total defeat. At the mid-point, in 415, came the vote in the Athenian Council to destroy the small island-state of Melos, because it refused to join in the war. It was not the command of a dictator, as we might expect, but a democratic vote in the city in which democracy was born.

Preceding the attack, the two sides had a meeting, recorded in great detail by Thucydides. The Melians explained that they had been independent for a thousand years, had caused no offence to anyone and would not give up their freedom. Thucydides gives the response of the Athenian delegate:

> *As far as right and wrong are concerned, the Athenians think there is no difference between the two, and that those states who still preserve their independence do so because they are strong, and that if we fail to attack them it is because we are afraid… Of the gods we believe, and of men we know, that in obedience to an irresistible instinct, they rule wherever they can. We neither enacted this law, nor were the first to carry it out… we merely avail ourselves of it, as you would yourselves in our place.*

Hitler proclaimed the same 'irresistible instinct' in our own time in *Mein Kampf*. There are strangely precise parallels, also, between that and Thucydides' appalled description of what was happening to the beloved Greek language in contemporary Athens:

> *What used to be described as a thoughtless act of aggression was now regarded as the courage one would expect in a party member. To think of the future and wait, was merely another way of saying one was a coward; any idea of moderation was just an attempt to disguise one's unmanly character. The ability to understand a question from all sides meant that one was totally unfitted for action.'*

From our point in history, we can see that that was the underlying belief of all empires, including the British at their peak. In the 1890s, they knew that if the small Boer Republic were allowed to secede from the Empire, the whole edifice might collapse. Since the Empire was by then a sacred value, a war to prevent it was sacred too, and men flocked to the colours.

They did not know that this was only an overture, and in less than twenty years all the empires of Europe would destroy each other. The ghost would struggle on. Hitler would see in Empire the chance of a world Reich, and Stalin would pick up on the same image. For both, the image of the whole, the *whole world,* would be at the centre of their fantasy. Throughout Western history, the same image has risen repeatedly and gone through the same ritual of self-destruction. Yeats described, in his own time, the same visitation from the same Dark Face of God.

> *Things fall apart; the centre cannot hold;*
> *Mere anarchy is loosed upon the world…*
> *The best lack all conviction, while the worst*
> *Are full of passionate intensity.*[2]

Thucydides recorded the Peloponnesian War as if it were a sacred duty to the future; and for him, Euripides was of like mind, for in the very same year that Melos died, Euripides put it on stage. The annual theatre in Athens was the greatest creator of consciousness of any human culture anywhere, but the people didn't always want it. Particularly, they didn't want Euripides. As always, he took his drama down to the roots of its action, which were in the founding image of Greek culture: the destruction of Troy. It opened with the great God Poseidon, grieving for his beloved city, and then cuts to a small group of women awaiting the ships, which would take them into slavery. Their husbands and sons are dead, their daughters bound like themselves, for the beds of their conquerors, and their city is in flames. One of the women is the great queen Hecuba herself.

Euripides is saying: 'This is the reality of their patriotism, perhaps of all patriotism! Just look, and *feel!*' And he spares

---

[2] W. B. Yeats, *The Second Coming.*

the audience nothing. Imagine ourselves sitting on the stone benches beneath the Acropolis, waiting for the latest offering from the poet. We are ordinary, patriotic, right-thinking people of moderate intelligence, moderate sensibility. Some of us are uneasy about the crime, so recently, of Melos, but not many. And Euripides tells us that the true meaning of our civilisation is sacrilege. When Poseidon plots his revenge, where can it fall except on us? The theme of sacrilege comes ever closer as the play proceeds. The Trojan princess Cassandra, vowed to virginity in the temple of our own goddess Athena, is dragged off to the bed of our own General, Agamemnon. Our standpoint in our own sacred ground is cut. And it is what they think of as their patriotism which has done the cutting.

Perhaps we are women sitting there, and we hear that the infant son of Hector is to be killed, lest he grow up to avenge his father. It is a very ancient argument, this. Himmler deployed it at the Lakeside Conference where he announced the Final Solution to the officers who would have to carry it out. There was some protest at the idea of killing the Jewish children. But, said Himmler, they had to go or they would grow up to avenge their parents. It was the simple logic of power that they should do that. Shakespeare used it in his own study of evil. Fleance must die with his father Banquo, says Macbeth. The social fabric is held together by Eros, and the fabric crumbles first inside the minds of those who are estranged from it. The more perceptive of the victims in the Nazi death camps knew that the worst threat was not to their lives, but to their humanity; and they knew also that their masters had already lost it. Euripides spares us nothing: he seems determined that we should feel that broken little body put into the arms of his grandmother, since his mother has already left on her long journey into slavery. Hecuba weeps:

> *Poor little head!*
> *Your soft curls were a garden where your mother*
> *   planted kisses…*
> *Now the blood shines through the shattered skull.*

She goes on to speak of that central act of piety for all Greeks and all Trojans: the burial of the ancestors…

> *You made a promise once, nestled against my dress.*
> *'Grandmother, when you die,' you said, 'I will cut off a*
> *   curl of my hair for you, and bring my friends, and*
> *   grace your tomb with gifts and holy words.'*
> *You broke your promise, son; instead I bury you.*

The meaningful order of the Greek world is upturned, the interplay between generations, the harmonious dance of life and death. That, says Euripides, is what your patriotic myth actually means: the undoing of the very fabric of Greek life.

But as the play went on stage, Athens was preparing for another such expedition, and on a much larger scale than Melos. Throughout the city, every man, ship, and piece of gold was being called in for a great attack on Syracuse. Thucydides again records the debate before the fleet sailed. The vain rabble-rouser Alkibiades argued in favour. His was once more the logic of power, the argument for the pre-emptive strike, and it went something like this: Syracuse is the most powerful city in this part of the world. It is in the sheer logic of power that one day it will attack us, so we must strike now. If we destroy Syracuse, then the other Greek colonies in Sicily and Southern Italy will join us, out of terror for what we may do to them. Together, we will cross the Mediterranean and destroy Carthage. Finally, all together, we will return to the Aegean and deal with Sparta. He ended with a great appeal to their greed.

Then think of the tribute that will pour into our coffers.

Nicias, the general who would be in charge of the expedition if it sailed, argued against it, on military grounds. It all depends, he said, on the first premise, the conquest of Syracuse—which is far from certain. The Syracusans will be fighting with courage and skill, on their own ground, for their own families and lives. The Athenians will be far from home, well beyond help if anything goes wrong; and if they fail, Athens will be stripped of men and resources and left quite friendless in the world.

The vote went to Alkibiades and the expedition went ahead. It was simply lost. Nicias himself died. Alkibiades did not die: other adventures awaited him. Yet the quarries from which Syracuse had been built filled up with Athenians, and no one knew how to feed them, or bury them when they died. Scarcely a man got home. Psychologically, Napoleon's plunge into Russia and Hitler's a century later were similar. The vast reaches of the Russian winter have been a magnet for any over-powerful tyrant in Europe, unconsciously seeking destruction. Even the salt mines in which so many of Hitler's men ended their lives were eerily like the quarries in which the Athenians ended theirs. Euripides saw it all but became, nevertheless, the most unpopular man in Athens. For at what point does an audience of ordinary, patriotic people of moderate intelligence, begin to shout, 'Euripides is a traitor'—just for knowing what they were doing to themselves, and telling them?

His last two plays were written in exile and performed after his death. If *The Women of Troy* is still the greatest anti-war document in any literature, it was not Euripides' last. *Iphigenia in Aulis* concerns the sacrifice of the general's daughter so that the fleet could sail for Troy. The other is perhaps the greatest play ever written, *The Bacchae.*

Iphigenia in Aulis

When the play opens, we are at Aulis, the port opposite Troy. The great expedition is gathered there: thousands of men, hungry for loot and wanting to get on with the war, and be home for the Harvest. But there is no wind: it is any general's nightmare. The High Priest says there will be no wind until Agamemnon sacrifices his daughter Iphigenia, who will soon arrive, on the pretext of being married to the great warrior, Achilles, but is actually coming to her death. All the values of house and home, everything which makes a living human culture are contained in this figure: Iphigenia. The High Priest is right. In order to destroy Troy, she must be sacrificed.

As the play opens, Agamemnon sits on a stage, empty except for a table and a lamp, scribbling a letter, crossing it out, pacing up and down, weeping, returning to his letter. He calls a slave and an old man comes on stage. What's his master up to now, he wonders? Why this agitation, these tears, this pacing up and down? And Agamemnon tells him the whole story — and tells it to us. He tells of the suitors for Helen, the most desirable woman in the world (so it was said), and of the pact her suitors made: that whoever was chosen would have the support of all the others in keeping her. He tells of the choice falling on Menelaus, his brother, and then of the Trojan prince Paris watching his herds on the mountain, to whom appear three goddesses, asking him to judge which of them is the most beautiful — that is, to judge, I think, *which of them represents the highest value*. There is Athene, the patron of the State; Hera, patron of the home, peace, and family; and there is Aphrodite, who represents sexual delight.

Paris chooses Aphrodite, and she promises him that he can have the most beautiful woman in the world. The latter is currently in the home of the Greek Menelaus, but, says Aphrodite, no matter!

So Paris sets off for Greece — 'seductive, perfumed, barbarous,' as Agamemnon describes him — and returns with the unresisting Helen. The Greek lords, answering the call and not averse to a bit of plunder, gather to fetch her back; and he, Agamemnon, has accepted the position of general and called his daughter to Aulis on the pretext of being married to Achilles — when what is actually planned is her death.

The old man, who is but a slave, says simply:

> *It's wrong! Stop it at any cost. Give me that letter quick*
> *and I will take it for you.*

And Agamemnon is persuaded, completes the letter he was writing and gives it to the old man with instructions to stop any carriage coming towards him that may contain the happy and excited bride.

Then the Chorus enters, and the plot becomes more complex. For these are women, and they are as enamoured of the war as any man. They tell of the great fleet lying at anchor, and of their delight in counting the ships, spying out the squadrons and the famous warriors at their heads.

> *What a sight beyond description!*
> *And how women's eyes love looking!*
> *We looked and looked, gorging on honey.*

Let's imagine it in terms of our own imperial culture on the eve of its self-destruction. A naval review at Spithead, with another just across the water at Kiel, where the Kaiser is building up his own fleet to make the challenge: battleships, cruisers, destroyers, corvettes, frigates, stretched in long lines; the royal yachts passing up and down, sailors cheering, pennants fluttering; and women lining the shore — lace shawls, silk parasols, big hats, excited chatter. They count the ships, mark the pennants, Admiral Lord this, Admiral Sir Somebody that, gold braid, medals, cocked hats; and always the women, beautiful, excited, admiring.

Then, from the Chorus of women, cut back to the messenger; and lo, he has been caught by Menelaus, who has read the letter and is enraged that his brother could even think of refusing the sacrifice which will take them all to Troy. And Iphigenia is still on her way to the real meaning of all this pageantry — death, torn entrails, torched homes, rape.

The play pursues its way with argument and counterargument. Menelaus sees the absurdity of trading a loving daughter for an unfaithful wife; feels suddenly what it is, he says, to kill one's child — which is what he is asking Agamemnon to do. Briefly, he is having a moment of consciousness. Achilles himself, the bait that brings her here, swears now to defend her. But the archetype of destruction is moving in this mass of men, stronger than any individual consciousness, and moving towards its completion. The mass of soldiers are hungry for loot, and far beyond any scruple about a girl. Even the great Achilles is threatened by his own men. At this point, with every path blocked, Iphigenia takes her fate into her own hands and resolves to die.

The masterpiece of Euripides' psychology at this point, is that she takes on the very value system that condemns her. She becomes herself possessed by the spirit of Father and Fatherland, and accepts the sacrifice of all that she herself is. As we have seen with the women's admiration of the great fleet, she may not have been far from it anyway. Now she wants to be as good as any man and give her life for Hellas. Even the shop-soiled platitudes of patriotism begin to drop from her mouth. One man, she says, is worth a host of women, for only a man can die for Hellas. The contra-sexual element in the unconscious rises up, and takes over her consciousness. This is Euripides at his psychological best; and as she mouths the clichés of war, it is as if she becomes its mouthpiece. She will die so that Greek women will be raped no more! She will die for 'freedom!' She will set Hellas 'free!' She was not born for herself, but for Hellas! She has performed the projection of Self onto the symbols of the State that will mark, now, the whole of Western history in a gigantic loss of human reality. Last of all, comes the vulgar, brain-splitting fantasy of empire:

> *Greeks were born to rule barbarians, Mother, not barbarians to rule Greeks. They are slaves by nature; we have freedom in our blood.*

When the knife falls and the blood pours down on the ground, it is no more than the confirmation of what has already occurred.

This is where the play, from its own inner dynamic, ends. But Euripides' son found the manuscript in Macedonia after his father's death, allegedly unfinished. It is impossible to know, but it seems that he wrote an ending himself. This was a not-unusual procedure, even in Shakespeare's time. But in this ending, like the sacrifice of Isaac in the Hebrew scripture, the sacrifice just doesn't happen: an animal is substituted instead, so there can be a happy ending and the fleet can set off for Troy to bring back honour and splendid loot. Iphigenia herself is carried off to serve in the temple of Artemis, but Artemis has radically changed her nature. No longer is she, goddess of Nature, guardian of small animals, but a goddess of war, hungry for blood. They sing to her:

> *Dread goddess, bring our army*
> *Safe to the plains of Phrygia*
> *And grant that Agamemnon,*
> *With Hellene spears to aid him,*
> *May crown his head with glory,*
> *And by his victory win undying fame.*

We cannot be sure of anything at this distance of time, but we cannot imagine, either, an ending less Euripidean than this.

The Bacchae

In his last and perhaps greatest play, Euripides brings us up against the fact that Elohim and Yahweh are opposite aspects of one Whole, and that it is only human beings who find it difficult to stretch so far, and must be at one end or the other. When Tiresias, the Merlin figure in Greek myth, explains this to Pentheus the king, the Chorus of citizens approve him. In no way, they say, is he speaking against Apollo, but it is right to honour Dionysus too as a mighty god.

It is because this is not permitted in Thebes, that the world slides into the chaos of the last stages, the central image, the king's head torn from his shoulders by his own mother. It is a metaphor for a psychosis, in which emotions long repressed into the unconscious, rise up and swamp the conscious ego. It can happen in an individual, but also in a whole people. In *King Lear*, which is Shakespeare's study of this phenomenon, it is the images of the feminine that rise from their hidden places and overcome him — principally 'mother.'

> *O, how this mother swells up towards my heart!*
> *Hysterico passio — down, thou climbing sorrow... I*
>   *prithee, Daughter, do not make me mad...*
> *But yet thou art my flesh, my blood, my daughter*
> *Or rather a disease that's in my flesh,*
> *Which I must needs call mine.*[3]

And when Lear finally knows that he will become mad, he knows too that it is because he cannot bend, cannot stain his

---

[3] *King Lear*, Act II, Scene 4.

'manly cheeks' with womanish tears. Ultimately, in the form of Cordelia, he is reconciled, though only in death. But there is no conciliation for Pentheus, the king in *The Bacchae*.

The play opens on the royal palace at Thebes. At one side of the stage is the monument to Semele, the founder-king's daughter. Above it burns a low flame, and around it are the remains of ruined and blackened masonry. Dionysus comes on stage. He has a crown of ivy on his head, a fawn-skin draped over his body, long, flowing hair and a youthful, almost feminine beauty. In his hand is the *thyrsus*, a stick which ends in the multiple seeds of the pine-cone, and represented, for the Greeks, the phallus. He sets the scene and tells the story.

Semele was his mother. She was one of the three daughters of Cadmus, who founded Thebes. Zeus came to her by night but said she must never ask to see him. It must remain a relationship in the dark. Her sisters mocked her when she told them about the divine visitor. A very ordinary, lustful man, they said, who crept into her room; and if she became pregnant they would all be shamed. Driven by their mockery she asked one night to see him.

> *'Just as Hera sees you… Please!' she cried,*

And was incinerated by the sight. These blackened walls, he tells us, are what are left of her house, and he, the child of that thunder-flash, has come back now to avenge her.

The Jews thought that no one could look on the face of God and live. Psychologically, it would be to take the infinite energy of the god into the limited space of the ego. It would break the rigid boundaries of the ego and make us what we call mad. This is the subject of this play.

At the end of the play, it will be the *sight* of the maenads sporting on the mountain that will break the king's ego-boundaries; and that is the moment of his dismemberment.

Zeus, in myth, comes either in the dark, or as an animal or bird. The god must always be veiled.

In many of the myths of Greece, Hera menaces some mortal female whom Zeus has made pregnant. Maybe anyone who brings something new into the world must be menaced by Hera, since she represents the order of the family, the stability which is so necessary yet always disturbed by the new. Zeus takes the child from the burning womb and sews it into his own thigh, where it stays until its time comes. And here we have the child, grown up and on stage, the child who is born from the divine fire, come back.

Dionysus continues the story. Pentheus, son of Agave, is now king. He has heard that Dionysus is his divine cousin but rejects him, calls him a bastard and ignores him in the religious rites that as king he must perform. Cadmus, the original founder but now old, loyally tends his daughter's shrine — but now the son himself has come. As a start, says Dionysus, he has turned the sisters mad, driven them out of doors and with them, all the women of Thebes. A great inrush of energy has come upon the city and the women are drawn back into Nature…

> *Their home is now the mountain;*
> *Their wits have gone… one and all*
> *Sit roofless on the rocks under the silver pines.*
> *For I must show myself before the human race*
> *As the divine son whom she bore to immortal Zeus.*

The city is womanless — no one to cook the food or look after the children. Like the coming of Christ in the Gospels, the coming of Dionysus is an *epiphania,* a showing of the god, and it has that intense reality which in itself judges the quality of our own, and either breaks its structures down, or strengthens them.

Dionysus leaves the stage, and as he does so, the Chorus enter. They are the women of the city, fresh from the mountain. For them, the encounter with the god has been a reinforcement of their own deep nature and they tell of the joy it gave them:

> *O Thebes*, they sing, *old nurse that cradled Semele,*
> *Be ivy-garlanded, burst into flower…*
> *Bring sprays of fir, green branches torn from oaks,*
> *Fill soul and flesh with Bacchus's mystic power…*
> *There's a brute wildness in the fennel-wand –*
> *Reverence it well.*

'There's a brute wildness in the fennel-wand.' In the *Prometheus Bound* of Aeschylus, Prometheus uses a fennel-stalk to carry fire to men. Fennel has been used to carry fire since Stone Age times. The fire slumbers in the inner pith of the stalk, and bursts into flame only when whirled about in the dance. It was used in this way in the midnight revels of Dionysus, and symbolised a particular sort of consciousness — the light that glows in animals' eyes in the dark (*'Tyger, tyger burning bright'*) and in human eyes, too, when moved powerfully by instinct. Reverence it well, they sing:

> *O what delight is on the mountains!*
> *There the celebrant wrapped in his sacred fawn-skin*
> *Flings himself on the ground surrendered,*
> *While the swift-footed company streams on;*
> *There he hunts for blood and rapturously*
> *Eats the raw flesh of the slaughtered goat.*
> *Hurrying on to the mountain heights,*
> *Possessed, ecstatic, he leads their happy cries;*
> *The earth flows with milk, flows with wine,*
> *Flows with nectar of bees;*
> *The air is thick with the scent of Syrian myrrh…*

> *And like the foal with its mother at pasture*
> *Runs and leaps for joy every daughter of Bacchus.*

This meat is one with the wine, the nectar and the milk; for which they need only scratch the earth, to make flow the white milk. At this point, Euripides' poetry approaches the same mystery as does the Christian in the Eucharist; but here it is the earth itself which is the Goddess.

It is now time, the playwright estimates, for a little light relief. Two old men shuffle onto the stage, clad in fawnskins and carrying the *thyrsus,* which they beat on the ground. They are Cadmus, the founder of the city, and Tiresias, the great shaman of Greek myth, Eliot's 'old man with wrinkled female dugs,'[4] who has…

> *Sat by Thebes below the wall*
> *And walked among the lowest of the dead.*

They have sensed the spirit moving in the city, and are off to join the dance. Cadmus stamps about, beating the *thyrsus* on the ground:

> *I could drum the ground all night,*
> *And all day too, without being tired. What joy it is*
> *To forget one's age!*

To which Tiresias answers,

> *I feel exactly the same way, bursting with youth!*

This is not biological youth, but the spirit of Dionysus himself, eternal. Like the clowns in Shakespeare, they bring the humour necessary for any approach to deep things. Now,

---

4 T. S. Eliot, *The Waste Land – III The Fire Sermon.*

they are on foot (it would be dishonourable, they think, to go in a cart); and as they hobble off-stage, the young king stumbles onto it, 'extremely agitated.' He does not at first notice them, but addresses himself directly to the audience:

> *I happen to have been away from Thebes; reports*
> *Of this astounding scandal have just been brought to*
> *me.*
> *Our women, it seems, have left their homes on some*
> *pretence*
> *Of Bacchic worship and are now gadding about*
> *On the wooded mountain-slopes, dancing in honour of*
> *This upstart god Dionysus…*

Then comes the prurient fantasy that will in the course of the play catch and destroy him:

> *Amid these groups of worshippers, they tell me, stand*
> *Bowls full of wine; and our women go creeping off*
> *This way and that to lonely places and give themselves*
> *To lecherous men.*

We see what is going on in Pentheus' own unconscious. The invasion by Dionysus is the rise of unconscious forces inside him, and they are pushing up into a very frail ego-structure. Pentheus has nurtured a great fear of instinct, and now he has chained up all the women, and will hang the foreigner when he catches him. Then he notices the two Fathers of the City clad in fawn-skins and his rage has no bounds. Tiresias answers him calmly, and delivers to him (and to us) the deep rationale of Euripides' thought.

There are two things Tiresias tries to explain to the king. The first is that the irresistible energy which has seized the women comes from a god who has for too long been ignored. The second is that it brings something with it from beyond the boundaries of space and in the same way as do the ravings of the Oracle at Delphi.

> *The Bacchic ecstasy, and frenzy,*
> *Holds a strong, prophetic element.*
> *When the god fills irresistibly a human body*
> *He gives those so possessed the power to foretell the*
>   *future.*

At Delphi, like the shamans in many cultures, the Sybil entered into a trance: and that dimension in which past, present and future are gathered in a timeless 'now.' The Bacchic ecstasy, he is saying, has this quality too.

The second thing that Tiresias tries to explain is that the fruits of Dionysus are the natural fulfilment, which is potential in all living creatures, and comes upwards from within. Therefore…

> *Dionysus will not compel*
> *Women to be chaste, since in all matters, self-control*
> *Resides in our own natures…*

He is trying to teach Pentheus the same ethic that Jung distinguishes from morality. Morality is the tribal rule book, the *mores* of the tribe. Chastity is the integrity of the heart.

Beneath this exposition for both king and audience is the sense of Tiresias that Apollo, whom Pentheus worships exclusively, and Dionysus are opposite parts of a whole, like inner and outer, or the daylight and the night. And that Dionysus is down below in the rhizome, and Apollo is above in the leaves and the flower, but both of them make up the plant.

> *Everything in the unconscious*, as Jung says, *seeks outward manifestation.*

That perception is also beneath the work of Euripides. At this point, the Chorus affirms Tiresias:

> *What you have said, Tiresias, shows no disrespect*
> *To Apollo; at the same time you prove your judgement*
>   *sound*
> *In honouring Dionysus as a mighty god.*

At which point, Pentheus reacts with a sort of panic. *'Don't wipe your crazy folly onto me!'* And at once, the crazy folly begins to break out within him.

> *Go, someone, quickly, to his seat of augury,*
> *Smash it with crow-bars, topple the walls, throw all his*
>   *things*
> *In wild confusion, turn the whole place upside down,*
> *Fling out his holy fripperies to the hurricane winds!*
> *The rest of you, go comb the country and track down*
> *The effeminate foreigner…*

So Pentheus and the guards depart on that business, and the old men and the Chorus are left on stage, in a mounting atmosphere of frenzy.

> *Before, you were unbalanced*, Tiresias calls after the departing king. *Now you are insane.*

The sounds of shouts and crashing walls come to us from offstage, while on-stage the Chorus, like a mantra against chaos, sing of the peace that is beloved by Dionysus:

> *Dionysus, son of Zeus, delights in banquets;*
> *And his dear love is Peace, giver of wealth,*
> *Saviour of young men's lives – a goddess rare!*
> *His enemy is the man who has no care*

> *To pass his years in happiness and health*
> *His days in quiet and his nights in joy.*

The natural unfurling of the rhizome is the gift of Dionysus, and Pentheus will not permit it. At this point, guards appear from one side of the stage, escorting Dionysus, and the king from the other. It is the set-piece in which the Greek theatre delighted. First, speaks the guard:

> *Sir, we've brought the prey you sent us out to catch;*
> *We hunted him and here he is. But, Sir, we found*
> *The beast was gentle; made no attempt to run away,*
> *Just held his hands out… telling us to tie him up and*
> * run him in;*
> *Gave us no trouble*
> *At all, just waited for us. Naturally I felt*
> *A bit embarrassed. 'You'll excuse me, Sir,' I said.*
> *'I don't want to arrest you; It's the king's command!'*
> *Another thing, Sir, those women you rounded up*
> *And put in fetters in the prison, those Bacchants;*
> *Well, they're all gone, turned loose to the glens; and*
> * there they are*
> *Frisking about, calling on Bromius their god.*
> *The fetters simply opened and fell off their feet;*
> *The bolts shot back, untouched by mortal hand; the*
> * doors*
> *Flew wide. Master, this man has come here with a load*
> * of miracles.*

We think of Peter in the Christian myth, set free from prison.

> *And behold, the angel of the Lord came upon him, and a*
> *light shined in the prison: and he smote Peter upon the*

> *side saying, Rise up quickly. And his chains fell off from*
> *his hands.*[5]

Euripides wrote long before Christ, but the same archetype is present, for when Dionysus is aroused, the normal expectation, that if you chain people up they will remain chained, no longer applies. Another sort of causality is at work. From this point on, we see that Pentheus has no defence against this stranger, and is increasingly deluded.

First comes a sort of repressed homosexuality:

> *Your shape is not unhandsome*
> *For the pursuit of women…*
> *Hunting Aphrodite with your lovely face.*

But quickly the flirting turns into irritation and rage, for he is no match for Dionysus and the only thing he has to call on is his kingly power, which he can't now count on. He orders his men to chain him up in the stables, but as they do it, the very buildings begin to crash and break into flames. It is a metaphor for the king's own mind. The repressed unconscious climbs ever higher and, distorted by its long repression, can only destroy. It is what possesses a mob at the mid-point of a revolution: a blind passion to destroy.

At this point, Pentheus returns, and there, opposite him once more, is his prisoner, free. At the same moment, a herdsman arrives back from the mountain, with another strange tale to tell. He has seen the women, but they were not as the king had led them to expect:

> *The leader of one company*
> *Was Antinoe; your mother. Agave was at the head*
> *Of the second, Ino of the third; and they all lay*

---

[5] *Acts*, 12.

Relaxed and quietly sleeping…
But modestly, not as you told us drunk with wine
Or flute music, seeking the solitary woods
For the pursuit of love…
They were a sight to marvel at,
For modest comeliness; women both old and young,
Girls still unmarried. First they let their hair fall free
Over their shoulders. Some tied up the fastenings
Of fawn-skins they had loosened; round the dappled fur
Curled snakes that licked their cheeks. Some would
* have in their arms*
A young gazelle, or wild wolf-cubs, to which they gave
Their own white milk… One would strike her thyrsus
* on the rock*
And from the rock a limpid stream of water sprang.
Another dug her wand into the earth and there
The god sent up a fountain of wine. Those who desired
Milk had only to scratch the earth with fingertips
And there was the white stream flowing for them to
* drink*
While from the thyrsus a sweet ooze of honey dripped.
Oh, if you had been there and seen all this, you would
Have offered prayers to this god whom you now
* condemn.*

If we take Euripides too literally, we miss his point. This doesn't actually happen, but he is describing something in the human mind which is the consciousness of Nature. The men have felt it, but they also have their orders. They try to catch the women and bind them, and those same women turn violent and the herdsmen flee; but the innocent cattle are not so lucky. The women fling themselves upon them and tear them into bloody rags.

At this point they have become identified with the Furies, the *'queens of terror, their faces filled with dread,'* to whom

Oedipus prays in Sophocles' *Oedipus at Colonus,* the last play in the sequence, who are the Kindly Ones, but also the Furies which avenge all insults paid to them. They are the great, elemental 'ministers of justice' of whom Heraclitus also speaks, who will punish even the sun if he oversteps his limits. They are present with these women now, with all the power of earthquake and volcano in their arms — and just as little discrimination, for they are no longer in charge of themselves; they are possessed:

> *You'd see some rib, or a cleft hoof, tossed high and low;*
> *And rags of flesh hung from pine branches, dripping*
>   *blood.*
> *Bulls which one moment felt proud rage hot in their*
>   *horns,*
> *The next were thrown bodily to the ground, dragged*
>   *down*
> *By hands of girls in thousands.*
> *Then skimming bird-like over the surface of the ground*
> *They scoured the plain, and like an enemy force*
> *They fell on Hysiae and Eritria, two villages,*
> *And ransacked both.*

The messenger is deeply shaken and confesses that there can be no greater god than Dionysus — which is what Dionysus came to establish. But it is interesting that the responsibility for *which it is* is handed back to the individual.

Now the god himself stands before the king, as Christ in the Christian myth stands before Pilate, and it is the king himself who is judged. We watch as Pentheus, like a poor, senseless bullock, is led off to his slaughter. How does it happen? What is the moment of change at which the tables are turned and he himself becomes captive? It is when Dionysus suggests that he go out to the mountain and *see* these women. In order to do that, it would be best to dress up as one of them;

and it is that counter-dressing which opens the door to the unconscious opposite within the king. It is the reality of the timeless energy, the *mysterium tremendum et fascinans*; and for him it is dangerous, extremely dangerous. It is safe for the women and the old men clad in their fawn-skins, but for Pentheus it is not safe. The deeper layers of the psyche, which have the lure of the opposite sex, have been long neglected. The ego is split by forces that in the healthy psyche are germane and kin to it. And what is good food and drink for others is, for him, poison.

So this most patriarchal of men is shown dressed in drag, identified with his own image of the feminine which is in effect his mother and his aunts. He adopts even a bizarre coquetry.

> *How do I look? Tell me, is not this the way that Ino*
> *stands, and my mother Agave?*

He doesn't have to wait to have his head pulled off: it is already happening! The mother-*imago* is doing it.

> *Wait now*, says the god. *Here a curl has slipped, not as*
> *I tucked it carefully beneath your snood!*

And the dazed king replies:

> *Indoors, as I was tossing my head like a Bacchic dancer,*
> *I must have shaken it from its place.*

One sign of the ego invaded by unconscious forces is this incongruous contra-sexuality. Another is the vast inflation that accompanies it. He thinks he can lift up the whole mountain of Cithaeron in his arms. One of the great limits to the ego is its sexual identity. Without that, all boundaries may be dissolved.

> *Could I lift on my shoulders the whole weight of*
> *Cithaeron, and all the women dancing there?… Shall I*
> *put my shoulder under this rock and heave the mountain*
> *up with my two arms?*

It is similar to the inflation which destroys even the most petty and domestic tyrants. Pentheus leaves the stage, but we soon hear of his end. He has climbed up a tree, the better to spy on the women, and they have simply pulled over the tree and torn him limb from limb. His own mother, Agave, pulled off his head and she comes exultantly on stage, holding the object in her arms. Only Cadmus, her father, has the courage to meet her, to make her look at what she carries and *see*.

He takes her through it as a psychotherapist might do it today:

> *Look!* he says, *whose head is that?*
> *It is a lion's head*, she answers, *or so they say it is.*
> *Then look again, look straight*, says he. *To look is no*
> *great task.*

And then she looks, and *sees*. Consciousness has at last broken in.

At this point in the play, it has come to its own conclusion, both dramatically and psychologically. It has said what it had to say. But as with *Iphigenia in Aulis* we have a long and seemingly false ending, but much more what the audience would be used to.

> *Have mercy on us, Dionysus*, says Cadmus, *for we*
> *have sinned.*

Cadmus, of course, was the one person there who had never doubted the reality of his daughter's experience, and had always tended her shrine. He is also the only one present who

84

can bring the truth home to his eldest daughter. An uncomprehending hand is writing this ending, with a sharp eye to the box office. The truth of Euripides is not what Athens wants to hear. It seems to me that the director has just edited out the pacifist, anti-war, pro-Nature content.

Both Euripides and Sophocles spent the last thirty years of their lives in an Athens continuously at war with Sparta. I ask the reader to imagine what that felt like, living with the ever-greater coarsening of the heart and language which happens in any war, as reported by Thucydides at the midpoint, the crime of Melos.

The two old poets probably attended the City Councils, in which the major decisions were made, with the war-party always in the ascendant. From their own podium each year at the Festival of Dionysus in the Theatre below the Acropolis, they fought it, and Euripides, the more outspoken of the two, became more and more unpopular, until at last he went, for sheer safety, to a remote valley in Macedonia, where the great *Bacchae* was written.

For both of them, the treatment of women in the Athens of that time was a blasphemy, a blasphemy against Dionysus who was life itself; and the Furies in time would be revenged on them… In the *Bacchae,* we remember, the women of Thebes have abandoned domestic duties and followed Dionysus to the woods. One of the men whom the king sent out to truss them up and bring them back is astonished at the difference between what the king bade them expect and what they found, which was women of all ages in an innocent celebration with Nature. But it was those same women who transformed into Furies so that the men fled, and the women fell instead on the innocent cattle and then on peasant villages all around. The moment of change was when the men tried to bind them. It was then that they ceased to discriminate, and just destroyed. The world was out of joint, as Hamlet will say of his own situation. That is what a great crime does: it damages the very fabric of Being. Dionysus himself, and the women who are filled with his energy, just destroy.

The deaths of both Euripides and Sophocles preceded by only two years the death of Athens itself and the descent upon it of the chaos which is figured in the closing scenes of *The Bacchae*. In 404 BCE, the war with Sparta ended at last, in total defeat, the confiscation of the fleet, the razing of the famous Long Walls which stretched all the way to the Piraeus, and the installation of an alien government. Very narrowly did the Athenians escape the destruction of their marvellous civic buildings, the massacre of the fighting men and the sale into slavery of the rest. It was what they had themselves voted for little Melos, for no other offence than not joining their war. Corinth and Thebes, of the league that brought them down, had voted for that solution; but Sparta, always in awe of the Athenian achievement, would not go so far. So a recovery followed, as quick and remarkable as that of Germany in our own time, with imperial fantasies dead, and Socrates, Plato and Aristotle still to come.

6 Oedipus

Oedipus the King

The Oedipus Trilogy of Sophocles was considered by Aristotle the best constructed of all the tragic dramas presented in Athens. It is Sophocles' answer to two great questions, What is a man? And what is consciousness? The name seems to be a play on the Greek verb *oido,* to know. If we go to the folklore surrounding King Laius of Thebes, we find that as a young man he had visited King Pelops (who later gave his name to the Peloponnese, so this is an ancient myth), and abducted his son Chrysippus, whom he raped and murdered for his beauty. Pelops had laid a father's curse upon Laius, that if he ever had a son of his own, the boy would kill him and replace him as the man in his wife's bed. Child-murder is impenetrable., and we cannot see or feel what could be the motive for it, perhaps a hatred of beauty itself as it comes fresh from the Mother.

But it is Oedipus' inheritance, and it is his name and nature to know it. He will take on what Laius himself cannot even look at. There is something redemptive about Sophocles' Oedipus, a mystery deepened for our own time by Freud's use of it for his own purposes.

So let us look at Sophocles' story. Laius, king of Thebes, and his wife Jocasta desire a son and heir; but none comes. Laius makes the long journey to Delphi to ask why this should be but he is not told why: only that if he does have a son, the boy will kill him and marry his wife. He thinks he can deal with this, so cuts out sex with Jocasta. But Nature is far too strong, and a child arrives. This is something, thinks Laius, that he can easily cope with. He takes the child, drives a spike through both his ankles and gives him to one of his shepherds with instructions to leave him out on the mountain to die. Problem solved. Or so he thinks.

For the shepherd is a natural man with natural feelings, and he disobeys, gives the child to another shepherd on the mountain, who takes him back to his own city of Corinth and gives him to the king and queen there, who have no son and bring him up as their own. They call him Oedipus, the Lame One, because his ankles never heal. (It is likely that Sophocles is being extremely subtle here, the lameness and the verb *oido* crossing on this single destiny.)

When Oedipus is grown up, the destiny begins to unroll. A young man who has drunk too much mocks him with being a foundling, probably slave-born. Oedipus knocks him down, but he *knows* there is something strange about his birth, and he *has* to know more, since knowing is his nature. He goes straight to his parents and demands to know. They, as is general with human beings, *don't* want to know, and they think that a flat denial will be best. But Oedipus is not satisfied, and leaves secretly for Delphi to ask the Oracle.

He gets the same answer as had his natural father, Laius, years before: that his fate is to kill his father and marry his mother. He, too, takes it literally and resolving never to see either parent again, sets off in the opposite direction from home — and comes to a place where three roads meet with a cluster of dwarf-oaks above the meeting-place. A man on a big cart, pulled by mules, with a band of servants accompanying him, blocks the road. A herald, walking ahead, orders Oedipus rudely out of the way, and the man on the cart strikes at him as he passes. Again, Nature takes over. Oedipus falls into a rage and when he comes round, finds that he has killed them all, except for one who ran away. Then he goes on, and in a few days comes to a city, which is in mourning for its king, killed in some unknown *fracas* far from home, and now menaced by a Sphinx, a creature with the head and breasts of an especially beautiful woman, the body of a lion and the wings and claws of a vulture. The plague is raging; people are dying all over the city. It is proclaimed that anyone who can answer the Sphinx's riddle can marry the queen and become king.

Oedipus, homeless, stateless, city-less, has nothing to lose. He goes out at once and finds the Sphinx perched on a pinnacle of rock.

> *What is it*, she chants, as soon as he comes within hearing, *which has four legs in the morning, two at midday and three in the evening?*

Nature again takes over, for he knows the answer, though he doesn't know how he knows: it just comes to him.

> *It is man*, he says, *who goes on all fours when he is young, walks upright in his prime, and in old age uses a stick.*

At which the Sphinx utters a shriek, falls off her pinnacle and is dashed to pieces on the rocks. Oedipus goes back to the city, marries the queen and becomes king. For many years, he rules well, the city flourishes and Jocasta bears him four healthy children, two boys and two girls. The fertility problem has been, it is clear, overcome. Then the plague comes again. It is at this point that Sophocles' *Oedipus the King* opens.

We are before the royal palace at Thebes. At centre stage are double doors; behind them columns, a pediment, an architrave, all the signs and splendour of that vital institution, the city-state. Before them is an altar. A procession of priests enters left. They are broken and dejected, and they carry branches, which they lay on the altar as symbols of themselves. Guards assemble; the doors open. The king appears. He is in his prime, majestic except for a tell-tale limp. This is Oedipus, the lame one. The audience sitting on the stone seats below the Acropolis at Athens, already know the story and, like the crowd at a bullfight, wait for the great, beautiful beast to meet the death which is decreed for him.

The first image is the city-state itself, with its stone buildings, its law, its mathematics and engineering—and the single human being who represents it and keeps it in being, the King. And in that first image, another is implicit, for they all know the story: the blind and bloodied beggar pushed out of the gates at the end of the play. The priests have come, now, to beg him to save the city. It is of course his job, and he has started. He has sent to Delphi and even now he awaits the return of his emissary, who is the queen's brother Creon; and indeed Creon is seen off-stage approaching, and soon arrives with his message. It is that the killer of Laius is still alive and living in the city. He must be found and banished; otherwise, the plague will continue. The simple brilliance of the play is that Oedipus, who, as king, is the symbol of justice and understanding—must follow up a trail, which leads inexorably to himself.

We learn the earlier parts of the story in the course of the investigation. Bit by bit, the scattered images are brought together, and in the end they make a whole: the simple crossroads where Oedipus kills his father in an act of passion, which is linked with the passion in which Laius conceived the child; the tenderness with which the shepherd disobeyed the order to leave him on the mountainside; the drunkenness in which the youth blurted out that Oedipus was not his parents' child; and now the rage with which a young man has killed an old one. They are all points at which the story moves on, not by conscious, deliberate actions but through the activation of something deeper. Sophocles makes him a modern man, his discourse sprinkled with references to mathematics, logic, empirical evidence, reason. And yet his fate is to know the reality of the Sphinx.

Sphinxes were generally made up of several different animals and were images of Nature itself. The vulture takes dead things back to the Mother, and it is she who asks the question that Nature always asks: What are you, man? To be human is to be conscious; yet, there is nothing to be conscious *of*, except Nature. The Sphinx in real life doesn't really fall from her pinnacle. Nothing in the psyche ever dies. She is only gone 'for now.' But very soon now, she will ask: who killed the old king?

In the play, Oedipus sends for Tiresias and asks him, in a very straightforward manner: who killed the old king? Tiresias is the blind seer, the Merlin of the Greek world who crosses all boundaries and is himself a form of the Sphinx: man and woman too, human and animal. He knows very well who killed the old king. He has always known, but he won't tell because he knows that Oedipus can't handle it—and kings have the power of life and death in the city, with no questions asked. So he keeps his mouth shut. And when in the end, Oedipus wrings it out of him, indeed he can't handle it. The just, reasonable, all-benevolent king becomes at once a petty tyrant. Tiresias is a fraud, he rants; Creon has bribed him. As often with men who cannot face a truth about themselves, he becomes a raging infant.

It is when Jocasta comes to reason with him and calm him down, as women do when violence breaks out among the men, that we find ourselves looking in on the secrets of a marriage. Together, they consider the accusation that he killed her first husband and that their marriage bed is soaked in blood. But if it was Tiresias who told him that, she says, then he can put it right out of his mind. For prophets *don't* know, and she has proof of it. Long ago, the Oracle at Delphi told her first husband that he would be killed by his own son.

But Laius, as everyone knows, was killed by a band of robbers at the place where three roads meet. And as for the child, he had been flung onto the mountain. So much for prophets!

It is in Jocasta's proof that prophets don't know, that Oedipus knows that they do. In that image, the three roads meeting, the cluster of dwarf oaks over the meeting place, he knows the truth. And now is the time for him to choose: consciousness brings choice. Until he had that knowledge, there was no choice: he had intuitions, but they just came to him. Now he knows for sure, and he must choose.

As king, he could quash the investigation, nothing easier: kill those who know too much, send it all back into the *unconscious*. Nearly every tyrant in his world and our own would do that. Instead, Oedipus follows the trail, knowing now that it will lead inexorably to himself. First, he sends for the man who escaped the massacre, and who, when he had come to Thebes and seen Oedipus already on the throne, had begged Jocasta to send him as far away as possible, *out of sight*. For he had assumed that the king would do the sensible thing and have him killed. Instead, Oedipus sends for him. It is his name, to know. It is like the *anamnesis* in psychoanalysis, the bringing back into consciousness of what has been forgotten.

While they wait for him, he tells Jocasta and the audience, the whole story — how, at home with his parents, Polybus and Merope of Corinth, a youth drank too much one night and blurted out that Oedipus was not his father's son; how he had knocked the boy down, but felt that there was indeed some mystery about his birth, and had gone secretly to Delphi to ask the Oracle. How the answer was that he was fated to kill his father and mate with his mother. Like Laius, he had taken it literally and determined to leave Corinth forever and set off from Delphi in the opposite direction from home — only to come to the place where the old king died. Every detail of that encounter he tells her and it seems beyond doubt, that it was he who had killed the old king. His only hope is that the shepherd will confirm that it was a band of thieves who killed the king and not one single stranger. But he knows it is a forlorn hope.

He still has no proof, however, that the man in the cart was also his father; and salvation from that part of the prophecy suddenly seems to come—a messenger arrives from Corinth with the news that his supposed father is dead, and the people are calling for Oedipus to return and be their king. If Polybus is dead, then the prophecy, as Jocasta says, is indeed all nonsense.

He breaks into a cry of scorn for all that supposed system of meaning which is behind the rationally perceived world.

> *So, Jocasta,*
> *Why look to the prophet's words,*
> *The fires of the future, why scan the birds*
> *that scream above our heads? They winged me on*
> *to the murder of my father, did they? That was my*
> * doom?*
> *Well, look, he's dead and buried, hidden under the earth*
> *And here am I in Thebes, and I never put hand to*
> * sword.*

But the relief is short-lived. The messenger from Corinth turns out to be the same man who brought him down from the mountain and gave him into the hands of Queen Merope; and Oedipus has to face the probability once more that he is not of royal blood, probably slave-born. Is he to publicise that? Jocasta cannot bear that people should *know* it. She begs him to stop. The shepherd too, begs him to stop. And the interests of State at this point, *require* him to stop. But Oedipus is discovering his humanity, and that is more important than any requirement of State. Whatever he is, he must *know* it. It is then that he makes a very wonderful cry:

93

Let it burst! Whatever will, whatever must!…
I count myself the son of Chance,
the great goddess, giver of all good things –
… She is my mother!

And then he goes on, that the moons are his brothers – returning himself to the ancient, mother-right world, when the moon was the measure of all time, and thus of all worldly reality:

The moons have marked me out, my blood-brothers,
one moon on the wane, the next moon great with
  power.
That is my blood, my nature. I will never betray it
never fail to search and learn my birth.

And the chorus have themselves been brought into that world and chant back to him:

Oedipus, son, dear child, who bore you,
 Which of the nymphs who live for ever
Mated with Pan, the mountain-striding Father?…
Or was it Hermes, king of the lightning ridges?
Or Dionysus, lord of frenzy

As this scene continues, it is as if the palace crumbles in front of us and both the pretensions and the touchy arrogance of kingship fall off him and there stands forth a majestic man.

But Jocasta is now terrified, beyond her power to bear it. She knows something that Oedipus does not yet know – that the trail leads in the first place, to her. She begs him again and again to stop the investigation, then rushes desperately offstage – while Oedipus continues with putting the final piece of the jigsaw puzzle in place. The shepherd who escaped from the massacre is brought in. At once, he is recognised by the man from Corinth as the same as, long ago on the mountain, had handed the child to him. The vital question is now: who did he get the child from? He comes out with it, at last. He had him from the queen, with orders to kill him. There was a prophecy, that he would kill his father. But he had pitied him and given him to his mate on the mountain, the man from Corinth. So there is now no longer any doubt about anything.

As the drama continues, the horror mounts; yet also the grandeur. Oedipus, none other, can carry it, and his stature grows as he takes on what is, as we have said so often now, his own name and nature, *to know*. What we have, in Sophocles' Oedipus, is a Christ-figure, despised and rejected by men but also their healer, for there is no healing except in consciousness. Jung spoke of that, late in his own life, after that near-death experience from which he had not wished to return. Only then, he said, did he recognise…

> *How important it is to affirm one's own destiny… an affirmation of things as they are, an unconditional Yes to that which is — without subjective protests… an acceptance of my own nature, as I happen to be.*

Oedipus does this, but the revelation, that he had bred children out of his own mother, is too much for him:

> *Horror of darkness, drowning, swirling around me*
> *crashing, wave on wave, unspeakable, irresistible,*
> *head-wind, fatal harbour! Oh, again,*
> *the misery, all at once, over and over,*
> *the stabbing daggers, stabs of memory*
> *raking me insane.*

It is the experience of terror, when the ego touches an utter strangeness at the heart of our being, an utter incommensurability with our daily consciousness. It is not rational. The children are healthy, his wife loves him, he has ruled well. The gene-pool of nature can tolerate a good deal of incest. Morally speaking, he was innocent for he did it unconsciously, did everything he could to avoid it. And on the psychic level, the daughter who is also his sister, the son who is also brother, are truths beautiful rather than otherwise. The father and son *'tangled all together'* is how we are, whether we know it or not, and it is far beyond the reach of the ego.

Dreams are horror-laden when ego consciousness can't treat with them, can't take them in. And yet it was the destiny of Oedipus to know.

> *All come true, he says, all come to light.*
> *Oh light, now let me look my last on you.*

He is determined to leave the world of the light and go into the darkness, in which these things may show their own form and shape and rationality. He rushes off-stage to the marriage chamber where, above the bed, swings the body of Jocasta — from which, as we hear from a terrified servant, Oedipus takes golden pins and plunges them again and again into his eyes. Maybe in the darkness he will learn what he cannot learn by day.

The second to last image of the play is of the blind and bloodied ex-king standing on the steps of the palace, where he had stood in the days of his glory, now leading into the last image of all: Oedipus saying farewell to Ismène and Antigone, those daughters who are also his sisters, before being pushed out of the gates of Thebes forever.

It is a common choice for those who stumble on a truth that is too much for them to kill themselves; another is to go mad. Oedipus chooses neither. He goes consciously into that dark world, moves into another way of seeing, which is that of Tiresias, the great shaman of the Greek world, and of the Oracle at Delphi, where the priestess sits over the passage upwards from the depths and gives voice to the messages that come up from that other dimension of Being, in which what we consciously will and what comes upon us as fate, are joined in the single reality which is our lives. They have met together and mingled throughout his life: in Laius' precautions against being killed by his son, which brings it about; in Oedipus' decision not to see his father ever again, which takes him to the place where he kills him; in Jocasta's proof that oracles are nonsense, which shows him that they are not at all. In such moments, human intent merges into the dark pattern of the Mothers, and becomes one thing. Such considerations reverse even our sense of time. Like Christ in the Christian myth, Oedipus takes the cup that the angel offers. For him, there is no other way of knowing — which is his name.

His destiny is shot through with the feminine at every turn. It is the mother who bears him and gives him up to be killed; the mother who has him given to her and takes him as her own; the slave-woman who suckles him in Corinth; the wife who marries him, but is also that same mother who gave him up; the daughters who are also his sisters, who will lead him in his darkness by the hand; the Sphinx who is all of them together and asks him the dread question: what are you, Man? And at the end of his life, it is the Eumenides, known also as the Furies, who avenge all wrongs done to nature, but who are also the Kindly Ones, to whose hearth he returns in the sacred wood at Colonus.

In Hebrew myth a goat was loaded with the sins of the people (which I understand to be all those little accommodations with Nature which break the Law of Yahweh) and either stoned to death or dropped from the top of a high tower, or driven out into the desert to wander — by which ritual, the people felt purified. What had really happened was that any small beginning of consciousness had been successfully warded off.

Oedipus has not warded off anything, and it is that which is his redemption.

Oedipus at Colonus

The desert where Oedipus will wander now is the stony roads of Greece; and people will give him food, for pity, but drive him on for fear of the curse that is on him. For he is famous for the incest he has committed, and whether it was on purpose or not seems to have no importance, so powerful is the *tabu* against it. His sons want nothing to do with him; they will soon be jockeying for the throne. His daughters go out to find him. Antigone will stay with him and act as his caretaker and his eyes. Ismene will go back to the city, but come out to find them whenever there is news to tell. And slowly his fame begins to spread, as a man who has suffered extraordinary misfortune through no fault of his own, and is no longer cursed, but blessed. At this point, the last play in the Oedipus cycle begins. The scene is the Grove of the Furies at Colonus, which was the birthplace of Sophocles himself. Athens can be seen in the distance. On stage are various rocky outcrops, and at the centre, a stone altar. From the left, a blind old man shuffles painfully on stage, led by a young woman. They sit down in the shade.

> *The great lesson that suffering teaches is acceptance,* says the old man.
>
> *This is holy ground,* says the young woman. *You can sense it clearly. Why, it's bursting with laurel, olives, grapes, and deep in its heart, Listen… nightingales, the rustle of wings. They're breaking into song.*

Oedipus the King ends with the blind king thrust out of the city. In *Oedipus at Colonus,* he arrives at a green place, with birdsong, damp earth and the entrance to the underworld:

> *The brazen threshold of the earth,*
> *the hill of Demeter, the steep descent,*
> *the threshold rooted deep in the earth*
> *by the great brazen steps.*

Spiritually, it is the place where the three roads meet, with the cluster of dwarf-oaks over the meeting place, where he killed, unknowingly his father; but transformed, now, into holy ground.

Today, Colonus is a dusty quarter of Athens, and there are no nightingales. Then, it was a sacred grove, with the holiness that we meet in any untouched piece of woodland anywhere in the world, where the same rich note sounds; and we don't know whether it comes from ourselves or the place itself, or from both together, like two birds calling; and what earlier shrieked of the great crime, speaks here of a last resting place.

Soon, a local man appears. He tells them they must move on, for this is sacred ground, forbidden.

> *Sacred to what gods?* asks Oedipus, and the man replies:

> *The ones that watch the world, the Kindly Ones,*
> *The Eumenides…*

And at once, Oedipus knows that he must not move on, must not move on ever, for this is his promised resting place.

When the god cried out those life-long prophecies of
  doom
He spoke of this as well, my promised rest.
After hard years weathered
I would reach my goal, he said, my haven,
Where I would find the ground of the Awesome
  Goddesses
And make their home, my home…
And now I know it, now some omen comes from you,
  my queens,
Some bird on the wing that fills my heart with faith
Has led my slow steps home to your green grove.

The Terrible Mothers are terrible no longer, so when the villagers try to move him on he moves a short distance, and asks that the king be told that he is here. The king is Theseus, of nearby Athens. The people are sure that he will come when he hears that the famous man of sorrows has arrived in his kingdom. They leave him in peace and settle down themselves to wait.

While they wait, Ismene arrives. She has terrible news. One brother has driven out the other and there is civil war in Thebes. But there is another piece of news as well. The oracle has changed its message on Oedipus: it now says that he is not a curse on wherever it is that he lives, but a blessing. So each side will want to get hold of him now, like those mediaeval cities that scarcely more than a thousand years hence will fight over the bones of a saint.

Oedipus knows this, and knows also that it is his own sons who have most distanced themselves from his fate, who will now try to benefit from it. Then Theseus arrives. He greets the old man gravely, and promises that no one shall ever force him away from Colonus. Then he returns to the city, and emissaries start to arrive from the warring sides. First comes Creon, the present ruler, who supports the younger brother for the kingship, and when Oedipus refuses to go with him, tries to take him by force — then seizes both girls and makes off with them, but Theseus' men arrive in time and bring them back.

Then comes Polynices, the elder son, exiled from Thebes and now returning, with allies from Argos, to sack the place. He begs his father to go with him, at which point Oedipus goes into Fury mode himself. It is as if he becomes himself a Terrible Sister, the inexorable justice not of any king but of Nature itself, which returns the poisoned chalice to its origin, which is always ourselves. He calls down curses upon both sides. Polinices knows that the curse is just and right, but cannot change: he has stepped in too far, he has become himself possessed by what is happening. Rationally, he could call off the war, but he cannot do it, cannot tell his soldiers, who are all there in hope of loot, that their cause is doomed and that they should go home. Antigone begs him to call it off but…

> *A good leader*, he answers, *repeats the good news, and keeps the worst to himself.*

Then a peal of thunder is heard, and Oedipus knows that the time has come. In these closing passages of the play, there is a great numinosity: for Oedipus has come home, and the Furies which hunted him have turned into the Kindly Ones.

> *Stop my children*, says Theseus, to the girls, who are sobbing. *Weep no more… it might call up the anger of the gods. Here, where the dark forces store up kindness both for the living and the dead, there is no place for grief.*

In the great ending, there are the Four, the two males, both kings, and the two females, who perform the priestly duties of their sex, wash him in water, clothe him in white linen and do the other rites of burial. As they finish, the thunder comes again and a great voice is heard, calling:

> *Oedipus, when are you coming, we wait too long, we must move on, move on!*

It is Zeus himself calling. Antigone and Ismene hide their eyes, and Oedipus, accompanied part of the way by Theseus, the only human being allowed to witness this end because he too is a king, walks into the darkest part of the wood, and disappears.

7 The Descent of Orpheus to the Underworld

In the mythic imagination of the Greeks, Orpheus was the first singer, the first poet and the first musician, and when he sang, all nature gathered round to listen. Not only the animals, but the trees and rocks moved into circles around him. As a theme, it was popular in the later Roman Empire, for it represented a different sort of power to the marching legions which had made the Empire. Orpheus was Nature's own, self-organising power, and in villas all over the Roman world, from North Africa up to Gloucestershire, we still find mosaic walls and pavements where Orpheus is seated with his lyre at the centre of a mandala, with all Nature ranged around him.

When he tried to get married, however, the auguries were not favourable. Hymen, the god of marriage, winged his way across the skies to attend this important wedding, says Ovid, but his torch smoked and spluttered and brought tears to the eyes; and when the bride Eurydice, went walking in the fields with her maids, she encountered the shepherd, Aristaeus, much given in his lonely state to rape. Fleeing to escape him, she trod on a snake, which bit her in the heel so that she died and went straight down to Hades. Orpheus picked up his lyre and followed her down.

His singing opened all the doors down there. Charon, the ferryman, rowed him across the gulf; Cerberus, the terrible three-headed hound who guards the gates, fawned over him;

and as he passed between the ghosts of those imprisoned there, all of them engaged in the empty and repetitive patterns in which they had already wasted their lives, his singing brought what they had always looked for and never found.

> *The bloodless ghosts were in tears*, says Ovid. *Tantalus ceased to seek the waters which ever shrank away; Ixion's fiery disk stood still, the vultures ceased to gnaw at Tityus' liver, Sysiphus sat idle on his rock and the daughters of Danaeus rested from their pitchers.*

Ovid's readers knew Tityus, Tantalus, the Daughters of Danaeus and the rest — but for us, who are they? They are figures drawn from the very dawn of storytelling, far, far back, when the human imagination was just beginning to think of separating itself off from Nature. It was like being cast out of the Garden in the Hebrew myth. Here, it was a state of being still on such good terms with the gods that they dined in each other's houses. Yet something was moving in the human mind: a groping premonition of some huge task awaiting it, to grow up and suffer the brightness of consciousness, which meant leaving the paradise of togetherness, which is a great blessing but also a great pain, which no other animal need suffer.

It is the subject of Titian's painting *The Flaying of Marsyas,* among the greatest of his paintings, and perhaps the last. The myth had significance for him, because there was some sense in which he saw Marsyas as himself. Marsyas was a centaur — that is to say half-man and half-goat. He had invented the Pan Pipes, which could be heard all through the mountains of the ancient world, for a shepherd need only cut a reed from a mountain spring, cut some holes in it for the stops, and he could become very skilled in playing it. Marsyas accepted a challenge from Apollo: that he could not make such lovely music with the pipes as Apollo could with that far more sophisticated instrument, the stringed lyre. Marsyas lost and Apollo pronounced his forfeit. It was to be flayed, stripped of his shaggy goatskin and made to share the nakedness of the human state, exposed to all the pain and beauty of the world. Titian paints himself in the picture, just watching. The executioners perform their task with a ritual detachment. There's something sacred happening here: symbolically, it is the making of consciousness, the opening of Marsyas to the almost unbearable beauty of what is in the world. And we know that the flesh that Titian painted so lovingly is this world — the fruit that Tantalus cannot reach, the water that laps about his neck which he cannot drink... What crime could have merited such punishment? Tantalus had tried to sleep with a goddess, great Hera herself.

Jung says in the *Red Book*:

> *If I could touch my desire and not the object of my desire,*
> *I could put my hand on my soul.*

Jung had learnt that. Tantalus had not, but we feel that he will; and Zeus kindly helps him along the way. He forms a cloud in the shape of Hera and lets him make love to that. And the seed drops down to earth, engendering there Centaurus and all the tribe of the centaurs, who were wildly sexual creatures, half-man and half-horse, embodiments of that fantasy that slumbers in the human psyche, flickers, flares up, dies down, is never extinguished, and seems to draw its power from an echo, drifting eternally round the world, of the great energy that created it. Ixion tried to make love to another goddess, and found himself bound on a fiery wheel, which spins forever through space, never touching earth. Sisyphus is yet another, who tried the same and finds himself pushing a boulder uphill, but has no satisfaction in doing it, for it rolls back endlessly, to the bottom again.

Tantalus is the most ambitious, trying to make love to Hera; but he also went even further: he invited all the gods to dinner and served up his son Pelops for them to eat. It is a most hideous image, and Ovid seems to take it literally. As symbol, it is like the Christian Eucharist but the other way round. There, God gives his son so that all men can be a little bit divine. The real point of all these images is the great, I think universal, myth of incarnation, spirit and matter married, partaking of each other. At Tantalus' dinner party, most of the gods are outraged by the offering. They have no wish at all to be exposed to the vicissitudes of the human condition. Only Demeter accepts a little bit of meat. Why Demeter? Because she has suffered as much as any human mother could: she has lost her daughter to the Underworld, and she had gone through the upper world howling her grief, until Zeus was forced to compromise, since all the corn was dying. Persephone, he judged, should come home for seven months of the year, but must return to Hades for the other five. And these two women would lead the way into a new sort of human being, one which would span the upper world of sunshine and all manner of beauty, and the darkness and death from which all this has to grow. It was the subject-matter of the Mysteries of Eleusis. It was said of those who had been initiated in them that they were immortal. By that they meant, I believe, that they had become conscious.

Nectar is sweetness, the sweetness simply of Being. The gods are eternal so they can never lose it — or have it either. We could say it is wasted on them, unless they become human, and that is the meaning of the great myth, the incarnation. It is why Zeus comes perpetually to human maidens, and they open to him; and why Mary accepts the visit of the angel and is made pregnant; and why all of us have such visits at least once or twice in our lives, for there is a pressure from the eternal, a perpetual knocking on our doors wanting to come in, into time and space, to experience birth and death.

If we come at last to Tityus, we must imagine a great giant, tied down over ten acres of land, his liver devoured by the same birds that eat the liver of Prometheus, the vultures. (It is a curiously specific image, that of neurotic human suffering, to be tied down and have your liver devoured by vultures.) The offence of Tityus was another attempted rape, this time on Leto, who was an ex-lover of Zeus and the mother of the twins Apollo and Artemis. Giants in folktales are huge and clumsy, with infantile passions, who dispose of the power of the volcano or earthquake. Tityus stretched on his four hectares of soil is like Christ on the cross and Wotan on the World Tree — but he is also like Caliban, who lusts dumbly after Miranda in *The Tempest,* and carries for that the curse of the father. But what can brute matter do, but lust after the delicate forms of psyche? And how can it possess them, except in imagination? It is there that Tityus has Leto, and Tantalus has the fruit. In the end, there is no other way.

The strongest of all these images is Tantalus, who gives his name to being tantalised. In all these incidents, he can see what, to the bottom of his soul, he wants; and all the world is showing it to him. Everything in Nature is saying it. But it is ungraspable. He can't possess any of it and that is the nature of his consciousness.

We return to Jung in *The Red Book:*

> *If I could touch my desire and not the object of my desire,*
> *I could put my hand on my soul.*

He is speaking there of this other dimension, the Soul, which the ancient storytellers knew, maybe better than we do. Tantalus is up to his neck in water, but unable to drink. I think that Titian experienced that: the almost unbearably beautiful world, with its landscapes and its human flesh. There is this clumsy but indestructible desire to bring both mortal and immortal together, without which the spirit can never know

107

anything, nor can matter either. Tantalus and Prometheus are the true heroes in the human story. They led us out of that time when the fire was still unstolen, Eve's apple still uneaten, when Plato's Androgyne had not split into the two halves that eternally search for each other—and men dined with the gods, and were as unconscious as they.

Ovid says, however, that when Orpheus sang, they were all at peace. Ovid was a poet himself. It was his life-long love. Another poet, Rilke, in the sonnet to Orpheus, wrote the line

Sein ist gesang. *(Being is Song.)*

When the song of Orpheus is heard, the longing of Tantalus and the rest is stilled because they are transported, if only briefly, into that other dimension, in which matter and spirit have come together and we are for a moment, in a full sense, conscious. That is why Zeus comes to human maidens, for it is only when the two sides come together, that the immensity of Being can burst upon them.

Failing anything so achieved as a true incarnation, there has always been an instinct to give something to the gods. That is the meaning of sacrifice, which seems to be universal. The Elgonyi, whom Jung met at the foot of Mount Kenya, have a strange custom. Every morning, at sunrise, they spit on their hands and hold them up to the sun. They don't know why they do it, they just do. But in this small ritual, the saliva, which is unique to every person, is given to the sun, and as it evaporates into its rays, it goes up to join it. It is as if the small sparks of conscious Being is what men have to give, and the sun needs it. In Christianity too, Christ offers his suffering to the Father, and the Christian is encouraged to add his own, as part of that gift.

As pointers to any after-life, Ovid's underworld is irrelevant, for it speaks too clearly of the condition of humans in this world. The myths of the Underworld are gropings after psychological truth. Ovid knew that they spoke of what underlies the conscious life, and that they spoke of it in the only language in which it can be spoken of, which is image. In his Underworld, there are those who have blundered too big-heartedly after the light, stolen fire or nectar, made ambitious but ill-judged approaches to god or goddess. And there are those, more numerous, who are tormented by Eros, tricked, humiliated, lost in a bog, caught in split-off patterns of energy, who don't change, don't develop, don't go anywhere. From these last, come the principal metaphor of the Metamorphoses, which is the transformation into a simpler organism, an animal or, like Daphne fleeing Apollo, a tree. The danger zone is always love.

Jung tells of a very old woman in the Burgholzli Clinic when he arrived there as a young doctor. She had been there since before any of the staff could remember, and had one incomprehensible symptom — to move her hands perpetually in a certain circling movement. The hand-movements seemed to remind Jung of ones he had seen in the old town of Zurich in cobblers' shops, where the cobbler would hold the shoe between his knees and thread, in just that way, the leather. When she died, her brother came to the hospital and the story came out. She had been disappointed in love with a shoe-maker, who, possibly realising what he was taking on, had withdrawn from their engagement — at which point, she had become fully psychotic and been admitted. The repetitive movements, thought Jung, were her way of keeping in touch with her lost love, not losing it. It is fully as terrible an image as any in the underworld of Ovid — an experience of loss buried so deep, that she did not know it was there herself, but which expressed itself in those endless movements of the hands.

Orpheus brings his music. The hunger pangs are stilled. The tortured circling ceases. It must be some form of the fruit for which Tantalus strains, the lost love of the old lady in the

Burgholzli Clinic, the longed-for embrace of Leto for Tityus; and of Hera for Tantalus. It must be some evocation of the whole, the *mysterium tremendum et fascinans* — the mystery that anything exists at all, let alone this world that hangs, as we see it now in the satellite eye, like a jewel in the blackness of space, wreathed in its veils of gold, green and azure, waiting like the bride in the *Song of Songs* for us to say the great words of the lover, which are actually the words of consciousness,

Behold, thou art fair, my love, behold, thou art fair.

Julian David
November 2019.

Select Bibliography

GIMBUTAS, Marija, *The Civilization of the Goddess* (Thorsons, 1994).

JACOBSEN, Thorkild, *Treasures of Darkness: a History of Mesopotamian Religion* (Yale University Press, 1976).

KRAMER, Samuel Noah and Diane WOLKSTEIN, *Inanna: Queen of Heaven and Earth* (New York: Harper & Row, 1983). This is essential for anything on Sumer.

DAMROSCH, David, *The Buried Book* (Henry Holt, 2007).

KAHN, Charles H, *The Art and Thought of Heraclitus* (Cambridge University Press, 1979).

SOPHOCLES, The Theban Plays.

EURIPIDES, *The Trojan Women*, translated by John Davie, in *Electra and Other Plays* (Harmondsworth: Penguin Classics). The most powerful anti-war document that the world has produced, but it made Euripides unpopular.

EURIPIDES, *Iphigenia in Aulis*, translated by Philip Vellacott, in *Alcestis and Other Plays* (Harmondsworth: Penguin Classics). The sacrifice of the daughter for war…

THUCYDIDES, *History of the Peloponnesian War*, translated by Rex Warner (Harmondsworth: Penguin Classics). The

Peloponnesian war lasted 30 years and destroyed the imperial ambitions of Athens.

OVID, *Metamorphoses*.

GOETHE, Johann Wolfgang von, *Italian Journey* (1816-17).

NIETZSCHE, Friedrich, *The Birth of Tragedy* (1872).

WITTGENSTEIN, Ludwig, *Philosophical Investigations*, translated by G. E. M. Anscombe (London: Macmillan, 1953). Lectured at Cambridge, but only published posthumously in 1953. Important, I believe, because he says continuously it is the world itself which speaks, by means of the image, not the logical philosopher. 'A proposition in logic,' he said, 'has no substance.'

JUNG, C G, *Memories, Dreams Reflections* (Pantheon Books, 1963).

ROVELLI, Carlo, *Seven Brief Lessons on Physics* (Riverhead Books, 2016).

About the Author

Photo: Emma Freeman Portraits

Born in 1933, into 'a Catholic family of exceptional piety,' Julian David grew up in the wilds of Monmouthshire. He had little schooling before going to Ampleforth as a teenager, from where he went up to Oxford in 1951 to read History. He came down in 1954.

> *After two years in London, trying to find a career in a world not constituted to my liking, I retired into a monastery and spent another two years studying mediaeval philosophy. I felt a need to go to the root of the modern world, which I knew was still in religion. In 1958 I emerged and began to teach in schools for maladjusted boys.*

At the beginning of the 1960s, Mr David started teaching at Dartington Hall School and married the painter Yasmin Wishart. They bought the remote and beautiful farm in South Devon where he has lived ever since.

In March 1969, under a new headmaster, Mr David set up a course of Comparative Religion and Philosophy at

Dartington. From 1970 to 1973, he ran the Dartington Social Work project in Sicily Project.

In 1976, Mr David came into just enough money from his Armenian great-grandfather to study as an analyst at the Jung Institute in Zurich. After graduating in 1982, he helped to set up the *Independent Group of Analytical Psychologists* as a new training institute in London.

In 1987, Laurens van der Post was looking for someone to be the founding analyst in a Jungian training centre in Cape Town, and chose Mr David. In January 1989, the Davids moved out to South Africa where they spent the next five years, through the end of apartheid and the first year of Nelson Mandela's presidency.

After returning to England, Mr David became Chairman of the *C. G. Jung Club* in London in 2006 and took on editorship of its journal, *Harvest.*

Mr David has lectured widely around the world, and continues to do so occasionally at Schumacher College and in Cape Town. He still lives in his Devon farmhouse, not far from his three children and seven grandchildren.

www.juliandavid.co.uk